FINAL MISSION

FINAL MISSION

The North Woods

Joseph R. Wax

Dedication

To the men and women of the Armed Forces of the United States of America who willingly and without question risk and give their lives in defense of freedom during times of war and peace, and the families that support them and the mission.

No story lives unless someone wants to listen.

J. K. Rowling

Why does the sun go on shining?
Why does the sea run to shore?
Don't they know it's the end of the world?
'Cause you don't love me anymore.

Why do birds go on singing?
Why do the stars glow above?
Don't they know it's the end of the world?
It ended when I lost your love.

I wake up in the morning and I wonder
Why everything's the same as it was.
I can't understand, no, I can't understand
How life goes on the way it does.

Why does my heart go on beating?
Why do these eyes of mine cry?
Don't they know it's the end of the world?
It ended when you said goodbye.

The End Of The World
Words by Sylvia Dee
Music by Arthur Kent

Table of Contents

Foreword

Heading north out of town on the two lane state road, at 50 miles an hour it's easy to miss the narrow sharp right hand turnoff, naturally gated by thick brush and tall trees. Those who intentionally discover and take this route leave the smooth pavement for the blue gray gravel surface, so often found on the many local backwoods byways. The loud chattering of tires along the surface fills the vehicle's cabin, punctuated by the occasional *ping* or *thunk* of an errant pebble being flung against the undercarriage. This road holds no scenic views, only the next copse of trees around each curve. It was built not for the many tourists or outdoorsmen frequenting the region, but for accessing and harvesting the region's rich timber resources. The occasional road grader or log skidder sits idly, standing watch along the roadside. If one dares divert one's eyes from the road at just the right instant, a fleeting glimpse of the mountain's summit flashes past. The gravel ribbon continues, winding its way ever upward, steadily gaining altitude and causing one's ears to pop.

The gravel gives way to dirt as the road steepens and narrows, becoming a two-way single-lane path. Travel slows as deep ruts staggered with protruding rocks create a bizarre natural obstacle course. Just as quickly, the terrain flattens and a small clearing comes into view on the left. To the right hangs a nondescript brown sign, attached by steel bands to the cross arm of a plain wooden post. Like so many site markers in this part of the North Woods, the sign is topped by a deceptively cheerful moose silhouette cut from sheet metal. The sign's muted yellow lettering unassumingly informs travelers that they have arrived at their destination, stating simply above the simple depiction of a plane's outline, "B-52 Memorial." It does not prepare the uninitiated for the impending journey.

(Photo by the author)

After parking in the clearing, one crosses the road and heads uphill on a dirt footpath. The forest canopy closes in overhead; although it is broad daylight, scant sunlight penetrates to illuminate the way. On the left, a large sign displays the Strategic Air Command (SAC) emblem and motto, "Peace is Our Profession."

(Photo by the author)

The trail continues to rise. A small shard of bent silver metal rests at the path's edge, curiously out of place in the silent, otherwise pristine woods.

After several more steps, more metal shards appear, some large, some small; most are scattered across the forest floor as far as the eye can see, while others remain suspended in the trees. All are twisted and torn. All are unrecognizable as to origin and purpose.

Stepping carefully over exposed roots and rocks, one reaches the heart of the expansive forest clearing. Far larger forms emerge from the shadows. The continuous rapid onslaught of imagery quickly outpaces conscious recognition. After an imperceptible delay, the mind clears with the realization that these shapes are the landing gear of a massive aircraft, surrounded by grotesquely deformed sections of wings and wheels, fins and fuselage, and finally, the bubble canopy of a tail gunner's compartment. Astonishment is but fleeting, as the bottom drops out of one's stomach with a sickening silent *thud*. The eyes involuntarily well and shed a tear, for on this hallowed ground, on a long ago frigid mid-winter afternoon, seven airmen lost their lives, two miraculously survived, and nine families were forever changed.

1

Prologue

The B-52 Stratofortress, colloquially called the "BUFF", an acronym for what some say stands for "Big Ugly Fat Fellow," was conceived in the late 1940s as the nation's first long-range high-altitude strategic jet bomber, designed for and capable of delivering nuclear ordinance to designated targets while flying nonstop, directly from the continental United States. Over time, various modifications were incorporated into a successive series of production models. Each aircraft series was distinguished by its alphabetical designation, beginning with the first operational aircraft, or "B" series in 1955, and ending with the "H" series in 1962. By the time that the last B-52 aircraft was manufactured in 1962, the Boeing Company had built a total of 744 B-52 aircraft.

The Strategic Air Command (SAC) of the United States Air Force oversaw two components of America's nuclear deterrence and response triad, specifically the weapons delivered by aircraft and via land-based missiles. The Navy provided the third component of the triad, nuclear submarine-based missiles to be launched from undersea. Thus, SAC commanded all B-52 planes and their crews. Though often grueling for the crews, these assignments were highly sought after and highly selective. Westover Air Force Base in Chicopee, Massachusetts became home to the Eighth Air Force, a major SAC command, in 1955. The 99th Bombardment Wing, Heavy (SAC), comprised of the 346th, 347th, and 348th Squadrons flying the B-52, was relocated from Fairchild Air Force Base, outside of Spokane, Washington, to Westover the following year.

SAC initiated a system whereby a number of bombers armed with nuclear weapons would remain aloft at all times, ensuring that not only would an external attack on the United States not obliterate all American nuclear forces, but would certainly in turn be met with a massive retaliatory nuclear response. Initially, at least twelve B-52s, referred to as "The Dirty Dozen," were kept airborne and did not land until their respective relief planes were in the air. Subsequently, more planes were brought into the program, the number of which at any given time was kept secret. These missions could last for 24 hours, facilitated through in-air refueling, while simultaneously serving to provide extensive crew training. The 99th Bombardment Wing participated in this program.

In addition to these duties, as of October 1, 1957, the crews participated in the newly ordered alert system. The program's goal was to maintain one-third of the American bomber force crewed, armed, combat-ready, and capable of becoming airborne within 15 minutes of being given the order. Fifteen minutes was the estimated time interval from the identification of an inbound Soviet nuclear weapon until impact over its intended American target. In actuality, the highly trained and experienced crews were often in their planes and ready to go in under two minutes, and prepared for takeoff in five minutes.

While on alert at Westover, crews spent twenty fours hours a day, seven days straight every fourth week living on base in a reinforced concrete bunker-like structure referred to as the "mole hole." Enclosed within a high-security section of the base and entered by way of corrugated metal tunnels, the building was adjacent to the flight line. After coming on alert duty and first ensuring that their assigned aircraft was "cocked," or mission ready, the men familiarized themselves with their crew's assigned target, anticipated weather conditions, and their specific individual assigned duties.

The crews' quarters were in the subterranean, windowless portion of the structure, which contained secure study areas, a dedicated mess hall, game room, and sleeping rooms. Television and movies were available, as was telephone contact with their families. The mission needs required a plane's crew to be in close proximity to each other 24 hours a day. Their movements were restricted to the "mole hole" or specified nearby areas on base while remaining in constant communication with the base operations center. At least once during every alert period, crewmen could count on being rousted by a loud klaxon horn at any time of day or night, signaling an unannounced alert drill and a rush to their designated aircraft. The crew, however, would not be informed that the exercise was in fact a drill until they were on board the plane. A code "alpha" required them to board and take their positions, a "bravo" would additionally require the engines to be started, while the rarely called "coco" had them taxi to the runway.

Many of the 99th Bombardment Wing's planes were B-52C models. Thirty-five B-52Cs had been built from October 13, 1955 through July 9, 1956, all at the Seattle Boeing plant, each at a cost of almost $7.3 million, the equivalent of $68.5 million in 2019 dollars. The aircraft was a behemoth, even by today's standards. 156 feet in length, the fuselage was longer than half a football field. The wings spanned 185 feet, and encompassed 4000 square feet of surface area. The unusually tall tail fin, or vertical stabilizer, towered 48 feet above the ground, equivalent to the height of a four-story building. The plane's full crew complement consisted of six men, including five officers who were seated in the bi-level forward crew compartment. The upper deck was occupied by the pilot and co-pilot, sitting side by side, with the electronic warfare officer seated just behind them while facing forward. The navigator and radar navigator (bombardier) were seated side by side on the windowless lower deck. A separate cramped aft compartment housed the sole enlisted crewman, the tail gunner.

Improvements in the C model included new navigation and fire-control systems, and a much larger external fuel tank on each wing's tip, which increased the tank's fuel capacity from 1000 to 3000 gallons. Additionally, the undersurfaces of the plane were now painted white to deflect thermal heat emanating from a nuclear blast. Fully loaded with 41,550 gallons of fuel and 43,000 pounds of ordnance, the plane weighed 450,000 pounds at takeoff. Its eight Pratt and Whitney J57-P-19W turbojet engines provided 12,100 pounds of thrust and a maximum airspeed of 636 mph. Cruising at a combat altitude of almost 46,000 feet, the B-52C offered a combat radius of 3305 miles, allowing the plane to travel that distance to a target, deliver its payload, and return home without refueling.

B-52C in flight. Note the distinctive anti-flash white paint coating the plane's underbelly and the large external fuel tanks on each wing. (Photo courtesy of National Archives, photo number 342-B-01-014-2-KKE10056)

Despite the B-52's intended purpose, the development of an extensive integrated Soviet air defense network consisting of radar, ground to air missiles, and interceptor fighter jet units, concerns were raised regarding the risks to the B-52 during a confrontation with the Soviets. One incident in particular drove home the stark reality of the issue. Since 1958, the United States had been conducting covert reconnaissance flights over the Soviet Union. The U-2 high altitude spy plane was developed for these missions, as it could perform at altitudes thought to be unreachable by Soviet fighters and surface to air missiles (SAMs). On May 1, 1960, a U-2 flown by Central Intelligence Agency pilot Francis Gary Powers was shot down from an altitude of 70,000 feet by a barrage of Soviet SAMs. This event demonstrated that the Strategic Air Command's nuclear-capable bomber fleet, of which the B-52 was the planned long-term mainstay, was now vulnerable to Soviet air defenses. The mission of the B-52 had, in short order, evolved from that of a high altitude strategic bomber into that of a low level penetrator. An adjustment in B-52 flying tactics was rapidly needed to adapt to the new threat.

The initial approach, high obstacle clearance flying, called for the pilot to fly at the lowest possible altitude that would ensure clearance of the highest terrain along the flight path. The lowest altitude, however, was often not low enough to avoid radar detection during penetration of enemy airspace. Moreover, the high-speed low-level flying associated with this technique was associated with much more turbulence than previously encountered at the B-52's originally intended high altitudes.

Subsequently, contour flying was introduced, where the plane's actual altitude would continuously change to maintain a fixed altitude above the every changing terrain features. Thus, pilots could follow the terrain at a prescribed height above the ground, as opposed to a prescribed height above upcoming obstacles. Contour flying was made possible by the development of advanced capability radar or ACR, also called terrain avoidance radar. The new radarscope offered a selection of 2 different continuous presentations of the terrain at selected distances of three, six, and ten miles ahead of the aircraft. The first visual option was a profile view of the terrain, while the second option presented an aerial map-like view. Installation of the ACR equipment in the B-52 fleet incurred a total projected cost of $313.2 million. Contour flying, though, exposed the plane to even more turbulence and structural stress than high obstacle clearance flying. As the new technology brought an entirely different approach to flying the bomber, the Air Force initiated an extensive training program for familiarizing the B-52 crews. The technology was scheduled to make its Westover debut in January of 1963.

Joseph R. Wax

2

The Mission and the Men

During January of 1963, preparations were underway to begin training Westover Air Force Base crews on the operation of the ACR system that would soon be installed on their B-52s. Command pilot Lieutenant Colonel (Lt. Col.) Joe R. Simpson and master navigator Major (Maj.) William Gabriel, already trained on the ACR and attached to the 39th Bombardment Squadron of the 6th Strategic Aerospace Wing, had arrived from Walker Air Force Base near Roswell, New Mexico to instruct Westover's standardization crews, which would then be expected to train the remaining Westover aircrews. Simpson had been a pilot since December 13, 1942 and a command pilot since December 17, 1957. During his career, he had flown 11,531 hours, including 2598 at the controls of the B-52. Gabriel, a master navigator as of June 27, 1960, had logged 4366 hours aloft.

Each squadron of 12-15 aircraft typically had one standardization crew. These crews, selected on merit and ability, served as both the instructors and evaluators of the other crews in the squadron, ensuring that SAC standards established for a given aircraft's flight procedures and operations were properly taught, and uniformly and correctly followed. Every crew in every squadron received such inspections and evaluations at least annually. Since three squadrons were stationed at Westover, each had its own standardization crew, while a fourth such crew served as the lead for the Wing, overseeing operations for the other three. Together, the four standardization crews comprised the Wing Standardization Board, more commonly called "The Standboard."

Each officer held an additional title referred to as a "rating," based on longevity and flight hours. As described by Lt. Col. Ken Snyder, USAF (Ret.), "A graduate of pilot training school receives the rating of 'pilot' and a set of plain wings. After ten years and at least 1800 hours of flight time a pilot receives the 'senior pilot' rating and a pair of wings with a star on top. With 15 years of service and 3000 hours of flight time he receives his 'command pilot' rating and a new set of wings with a wreath around the star." The navigators, radar navigators, and electronic warfare officers received ratings as well, progressing from navigator to senior navigator to master navigator.

Beginning on January 21, 1963, the Westover standardization crews ran through six hours of training provided by Simpson and Gabriel, listening to lectures and sitting in darkened rooms watching films and slide presentations. The navigators and radar navigators trained on ground simulators to become familiar with both the ACR operation and the imagery produced by the radarscopes. Outside of the classrooms, flyers pored over freshly published supplements to their flight and technical manuals for the new equipment, further becoming acquainting with the ACR.

In order to maximize the efficiency of completing actual airborne training and gaining hands on experience with the ACR, the decision was made not to fly individual missions by each individual crew. Rather, two sets of the actual equipment users-the pilot and radar navigator- representing two separate crews would fly a single mission together and take turns operating the ACR, while supervised by the two New Mexico–based instructors. In contrast to usual flight operations, where the pilot took course directions from the navigator, during the ACR training portion of the mission, the pilot would take direction from the radar navigator. Additionally, since the pilot was using the ACR to guide his flying, the co-pilot would monitor the flight instruments and act as a lookout using direct vision while the navigator would continue to plot the flight path.

The first such flight east of the Mississippi was scheduled at Westover for January 24, 1963. The assigned aircraft was a B-52C, serial number 53-0406. 0406 had rolled off the Boeing assembly line in Seattle, Washington on February 29, 1956 and was delivered to the Air Force six months later on August 22. Prior to takeoff on January 24, the aircraft had recorded 2904.3 hours of flight time, 226.6 of which had elapsed since its last maintenance overhaul on October 10, 1962 at the Oklahoma City Air Materiel Area at Tinker Air Force Base, and 5.6 hours since its last periodic inspection. The

Air Force crew picking up the plane following the overhaul was informed of some corrosion that had been identified in the tail section.

Mission orders were issued on January 23, designating Lt. Col. Dante "Dan" Eugene Bulli, Chief of the Wing Standardization Division, 99th Bombardment Wing, Heavy (SAC) as the aircraft commander. Members of his usual air crew, Select (S)-O6, also scheduled to fly were navigator Captain (Capt.) Herbert "Herb" Lawrence Hanson, radar navigator Maj. Robert "Bob" James Hill, Jr., and gunner Technical Sergeant (TSgt.) Michael "Mike" Francis O'Keefe. The remaining complement of fliers was added at the last minute after their originally planned flight for January 25 was cancelled due to equipment issues. Representing the second crew contributing fliers to the mission, Select (S)-47, were the flight's co-pilot Maj. Robert "Bob" James Morrison, navigator Capt. Gerald "Jerry" Jay Adler, and radar navigator Capt. Charles "Charlie" Gerson Leuchter. All Westover crew were assigned to the 348th Bombardment Squadron.

Dan Bulli was born July 17, 1922 to Italian immigrants who had settled in the small Illinois town of Cherry and labored in the local coal mine. His father, John, instilled in him a love of the outdoors, passing on the skills necessary to become an adept hunter and fisherman. Dan, fascinated by aircraft from a young age, had his destiny sealed in 1928 after receiving a treat from his father in the form of a short flight with a barnstormer over Cherry. Bulli left home in July 1940 and headed to Los Angeles, where he was hired by Lockheed as an assembly line worker.

Following Pearl Harbor, with mixed feelings, he realized that he might soon have the opportunity to achieve his life's goal of becoming a pilot. However his job at Lockheed was designated a "reserved occupation" thereby exempting him from military service. Dan only complied with this situation until late 1942 when he could no longer restrain his desire to fly, enlisting, and earning his pilot's wings on December 5, 1943. At first, he was assigned to the Air Transport Command, ferrying new planes to where they were needed for the war effort, quickly becoming proficient at flying a variety of planes with little advance notice.

Newly-minted Second Lieutenant Dante Bulli (far left) with a B-26 Marauder, his all-time favorite plane. Lake Charles Army Airfield, Louisiana, late 1944. (Photo courtesy of John Bulli)

The Army Air Corps finally acquiesced to Bulli's repeated requests for a combat assignment in 1945, but the war ended while he was training on the B-32 bomber. He remained on active duty, committing to the newly formed Air Force as his career, and marrying fellow Cherry native Evelyn "Ev" Lewis in 1947. Dan later saw service during the Korean War on the B-29. A 1953 transfer to the Strategic Air Command was accompanied by flying its large bombers, the B-29 at first, later the B-36, B-47, and eventually the B-52.

Bulli family Christmas card, 1963. Marilyn and Sniffer (front row), John, Evelyn, and Dan (lt. to rt., back row). (Photo courtesy of John Bulli)

He and his family, which by now included two young children, John and Marilyn, were assigned to the 99th Bombardment Wing, Heavy (SAC) based out of Westover in the spring of 1957. On December 18, 1958, Bulli's rating was elevated to command pilot. He and his Westover flight crews were later featured in articles on SAC operations in the March 14, 1960 issue of *Time* magazine and the September 1961 issue of *Men* magazine. Bulli was regarded as one of SAC's top pilots, no nonsense and "by the book". With admiration, one of his fellow officers later described him "as tough as nails". His last flight prior to the ACR training mission was on January 2, and brought his career cumulative flying time to 7587 hours, 3039 of which were at the controls of the B-52.

Herb Hanson was born February 9, 1920 and raised in Chicago, the oldest of three boys born to Henry and Clara Hanson. His father was of Norwegian descent and worked for a printing press manufacturer, assembling and installing printing presses for new customers. His mother, born to German immigrants, died from complications following surgery when Herb was just nine years old. Henry's frequent work-related travels prevented him from adequately caring for his three active boys. Herb's two younger brothers, Jim, six, and Bob, five, were adopted by Clara's sister and her husband. Herb's grandmother helped raise him, although he remained with his father. Despite living in different households, the boys remained close and were together often.

Hanson enlisted in the Army Air Corps on May 27, 1943 and was commissioned as a Second Lieutenant on November 4, 1944. Trained as a bombardier, his first duty station was the Rapid City, South Dakota Army Air Base. It was there that he met and married local native Wanda Dean, who had served in the Women's Air Corps. At the war's close, the Army Air Corps, having accessioned more men than required for peacetime duty, discharged Herb from active duty on December 9, 1945. He and Wanda returned to South Dakota, settling in Deadwood, with Herb working as a short order cook at the Bodega Café, where he and Wanda developed many close friendships.

When he learned that the Department of Defense would designate the Air Force as an independent branch of the military, Hanson saw the opportunity to make a career of flying, a dream he had held since high school. After a celebratory send off by his friends and coworkers at the restaurant, he was reactivated by the Air Force on October 31, 1946. In his pocket, Herb carried their gift, a silver lighter engraved with his initials, HLH, on one side, and the salutation "Remember the Bodega gang" on the other side.

Wanda and Capt. Herb Hanson shortly after arriving at Westover AFB, 1957. (Photo courtesy of Deana and Gary Packingham)

16

The Hansons had three daughters, Deana, Patricia "Trish," and Samantha "Sam." Deana remembers, " He always had his camera with him and ready. It used to drive Trish and I crazy, as he loved shooting pictures of us. His three daughters were a precious commodity to him. He would always bring his girls dolls from whatever country he was in… Japan, Guam, many others. He once got me a GI Joe doll…I still have it." Highly organized, in preparation for these frequent deployments, Herb ensured that Wanda, who was not quite so organized, was provided with the means and information that she needed to continue managing the busy household. "Dad also loved dogs. He got a basset hound and named him Morgan Royal. When Dad was home…the dog minded only Dad. When Dad was gone, he minded no one. One day he grabbed an entire ham off the counter and devoured it. I think Mom took a yardstick after the dog. Dad heard all about it."

Moraha Dean (Wanda's Hanson's mother, lt.), Trish Hanson(rt.), and Morgan Royal, undated. (Photo courtesy of Samantha Hanson)

Deana, Trish (standing, lt. to rt.), Sam, and Wanda Hanson (sitting, lt. to rt.), 1964. (Photo courtesy of Deana and Gary Packingham)

Sam, the youngest, would often await Herb's return to their off-base home, sitting on a log near the curb. She knew that there was a pretty good chance that he would invite her to hop into his robin's egg blue Austin Healy Sprite convertible for a spin to the local A&W Root Beer drive-in for a "baby root beer." Regarding the convertible, Deana always wondered, "How he ever got in and out of it was a mystery...he stood 6 feet 3 inches." His daughters all appreciated his love of the holidays. He took great pains to ensure that Halloween included festively carved jack o lanterns. Decorating the Christmas tree was an annual family highlight, led by Herb. All shared in ensuring that it was a decorative showcase, so much so that one year Sam was awarded the second of three spankings she received over her lifetime, when, "in a fit of jealousy I tried to hit neighbor Wirth's Christmas tree with a broom. It was up first!"

They all recognized his characteristic patience, whether teaching Deana how to ride her first bike, or managing young Sam's occasional unpredictability. Sam recalled rebelling against her grandmother's attempt to perform a "home perm" with her hair. She left the house and headed two doors down the block to the Wirths, a fellow Air Force family and close friends of the Hansons, to see their daughter, her playmate Mary Bridget, or "Didge." "Thing was, I left a trail of clothing down the sidewalk. Dad was right behind me. He wrapped me in a crocheted afghan, threw me over his shoulder, and took me home. After I was dressed, he escorted me to Didge's house."

While at Westover, at the end of each school year, Herb would drive across country with Wanda and the girls to Rapid City. He would fly back to

Westover, while the rest of the family spent the summer with Wanda's parents, Moraha and Fred Dean. The highlight of their visit was the weeklong trail rides on horseback through the Black Hills, coordinated by Wanda's parents and their family business, Pretty Pines Catering House. By January 24, 1963 Herb Hanson, who held a master navigator rating as of February 10, 1960, had accumulated 4542 hours experience navigating the skies with the Air Force.

Capt. Herb Hanson, center, next to Maj. Bob Hill (rt.). This January 1963 is the last known photo of Hanson and Hill before their flight on 0406. (Photo courtesy of Deana and Gary Packingham)

Bob Hill was a Joplin, Missouri native born on June 12, 1925, who saw duty in the Pacific during World War II as a bombardier aboard the B-29, flying missions over the Japanese homeland islands. After the war, he returned home, first working as a meat cutter and then as a truck driver before rejoining the military and the Air Force. His sister, Opal Faye Boyd, would reminisce, "He loved flying more than anything. He'd rather fly than eat." He and fellow Joplin native Mildred Krudwig married in 1948.

Portrait of Bob Hill, undated. (Photo courtesy of Roberta Hill)

Daughter Roberta "Bobbie" Lee joined the family a year later and was the focus of much of Bob's attentions. She noted, "We had lots of good memories from the 1950's, like going to Disneyland right after it opened, with many rides still under construction, and going to the very first McDonald's while in California. We visited Yosemite, the Painted Desert, various caverns, and so many other locations when going base to base. I still have one of the striped rocks that Dad and I gathered on our trips. I also still have his roll top desk and chair he had as a child in the 30's, our minnow bucket from fishing in the 50's, his bowling bag from the 60's, and our ball gloves and baseball that we enjoyed so much."

Bob and Bobbie Hill cooling off in the Nebraska summer heat, undated. (Photo courtesy of Roberta Hill)

Bob, Bobbie, and Mildred Hill (left to right) at the family farm in Joplin, Missouri, 1962. (Photo courtesy of Roberta Hill)

A keen sportsman, Hill played both shortstop and second base for his Westover baseball club, aptly named "The Bombers", and taught the skills of the game to his daughter. A dedicated bowler himself, Bob coached and chauffeured Bobbie's travelling team, which additionally included four boys. He taught her to box and even bought her her very own gloves and punching bag. Together, father and daughter would canoe and fish. Bobbie "always enjoyed it when the crew came over to play poker, because I usually played a few hands with them." She recalled that "we would go out late at night and he would show me constellations through our telescope and talk about navigating by the stars."

The Westover Bombers baseball team. Shortstop/second baseman Bob Hill is in the back row, far right, undated. (Photo courtesy of Roberta Hill)

Hill's earlier role as a bombardier had evolved with the times. He was trained as a radar navigator on the B-47, and later the B-52. Bob had been assigned to Westover since 1958, accumulating a total of 3921 hours as a bombardier and radar navigator and held the rating of master navigator since November 9, 1961.

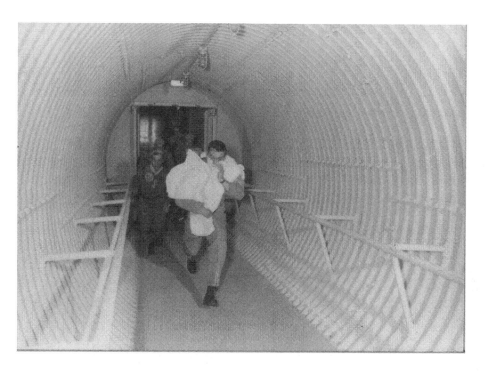

Crew exiting the "mole hole" during an alert drill. Capt. Herb Hanson is leading the way after being caught shaving when the klaxon sounded. Maj. Bob Hill, wearing ball cap, is just behind and to the left of Hanson in the image, undated. (Photo courtesy of Roberta Hill)

Mike O'Keefe was the fourth of John and Anna May (Joyce) O'Keefe's five children. Born August 19, 1936 to the two Irish immigrants and raised in the Bronx borough of New York City, he was also the youngest and only unmarried crewmember assigned to 0406. John Sr. was a construction foreman and Anna was a homemaker. At Grace Dodge High School, Mike served as Class President and President of Senior Activities. He played basketball and worked after school. Uncertain of his future plans, O'Keefe looked to his two older brothers, Richard and John Jr., who were both Air Force veterans, having served during the Berlin Airlift and Korean War, respectively. He recalled the awe that he experienced during his first airline flight with his father, an overseas trip to visit family in Ireland. The September following graduation, he enlisted in the Air Force, looking forward to flying and learning an employable technical skill.

Michael O'Keefe alongside an RB-52B, 1958. (Photo courtesy of Theresa Bailey)

Instead, the brown-haired, blue-eyed New Yorker who was quick to quip in an imitation Irish brogue, found a career. His superiors quickly recognized Mike's work ethic, intellect, and good nature. He graduated first in his class at electronics school and was immediately assigned to a SAC base. Gunnery school soon followed, after which Mike became a tail gunner on the B-36, and later the B-52. After completing his initial service obligation, he signed up for another six years. In just eight years, he rose rapidly through the enlisted ranks and was hand-selected to join the chief of standardization's crew at Westover, ahead of others more senior in rank and with longer time in service. It was no surprise that Michael O'Keefe's ascendancy was the subject of Arnold Brophy's 1959 monograph "Sky Sentry – A SAC Crewman in Service."

O'Keefe had just returned to Westover several days earlier, coming off of bereavement leave. His father, a World War I veteran, had passed away on January 13, 1963. Mike headed home to mourn with his family and attend the funeral at the Long Island National Cemetery in Farmingdale, New York. While the decision to head to New York was an easy one, it required him to voluntarily withdraw from Westover's Noncommissioned Officer Academy, a highly selective training program for up and coming technical sergeants representing the next generation of enlisted Air Force leaders. Upon his arrival back in Chicopee, he resumed his flight and administrative duties while awaiting reassignment to the next academy class. After just over eight years in the service, O'Keefe had spent 2278 hours in the air.

Bob Morrison was born on November 20, 1926 in Hutchison, Kansas to James, an auto mechanic in Dodge City, and Lena, a homemaker. Bob and his twin brother, Richard, were the youngest of the five Morrison children. At a young age, Bob's academic gifts were quickly apparent and he graduated high school at age 16 after skipping a grade. Despite their young ages, Bob and Richard enlisted in the Navy during WWII. Bob served aboard a destroyer in the Pacific, while Richard became a "frogman," a member of an underwater demolition team and precursor to today's elite SEAL (SEa, Air, Land) teams.

Robert Morrison as a Captain, undated. (Photo courtesy of Shari Morrison Hovey)

At the war's conclusion, Morrison headed home to Kansas, at first following in his father's footsteps as an auto mechanic. Growing restless, he joined the nascent Air Force, attending flight school in San Antonio and Lubbock, Texas. While in flight school, he married Irene Hostetler Mowday in 1949 and adopted her two children, Sharan "Shari," age 4 ½, and Robert Max "Max," age 3. Graduating in 1950, Bob was awarded his wings and commissioned as a Second Lieutenant. He was stationed in Okinawa during the Korean War, during which time his family temporarily resettled close to family in Dodge City.

Morrison at the flight controls, undated. (Photo courtesy of Shari Morrison Hovey)

Following his return stateside, Morrison and his family were stationed at numerous commands across the country before coming to Westover. Shari appreciated that "our education was not just attending school, but my father and mother made sure that wherever we were stationed, we would learn about and visit as much of the new area as possible. It was great." Max described Bob as "firm but fair, a model dad." Bob was a religious man and an accomplished, self-taught guitarist. He deeply valued time with his family, filling precious moments together with outdoor sporting activities.

Max, Shari (standing, lt. to rt.), Irene, and Bob Morrison (sitting, lt. to rt.), undated. (Photo courtesy of Shari Morrison Hovey)

The Morrisons arrived at Westover in 1959. In the summer months, as Commodore of the Albatross Boat Club at Westover, he could be found on the water in the family motorboat, towing the kids on water skis along the Connecticut River. There was also the occasional fishing trip to Minnesota and during the winter, there were family ski trips to New Hampshire and Vermont. He obtained his senior pilot rating on September 16, 1957. When he touched down after his previous flight on January 9, Bob had flown 5655 hours, including 2218 hours at the controls of the B-52.

Bob and Irene Morrison on a family ski trip, undated. (Photo courtesy of Shari Morrison Hovey)

Jerry Adler, a Brooklyn, New York native, was born on December 7, 1931 and was a 1953 graduate of Cornell University. At the time of his attendance, Cornell required two years of Reserve Officer Training Corps (ROTC) for all enrolled students. After two years, Adler decided to complete four years of ROTC and pursue an Air Force career. Following graduation from Cornell, Jerry excelled in his continued Air Force training, which included the Air War College at Maxwell Air Force Base, Alabama. He and Texas native Sonya, "Sonnie," married in 1954, with daughter Sheree joining the family the next year, followed by Karen in 1958.

Capt. Jerry Adler, February 1964. (Photo courtesy of Theresa Bailey)

Through early 1959, he was trained on the B-52, after which he joined a combat-ready squadron assigned to Biggs Air Force Base, Texas. In 1960, Jerry was promoted to instructor. The following year, he moved into the wing's standardization division and joined the senior standardization crew on November 27, 1961. When a position opened for an instructor navigator at Westover, Adler requested and was granted the transfer he sought to be closer to his New York-based family.

Jerry and Sonya Adler with daughters Sheree (lt.) and Karen (rt.), 1964. (Photo courtesy of Karen Adler)

The Adlers arrived at Westover in July 1962. Jerry and Radar Navigator Charlie Leuchter soon became roommates, sharing a duty room in the "mole hole" when their crew pulled alert. When he boarded 0406, Jerry had already flown 2582 hours with the Air Force and held the rating of senior navigator.

Charlie Leuchter, born September 5, 1930, was the second Bronx native aboard that day. His upbringing was not an easy one. Leuchter's father, who had been orphaned at an early age, died unexpectedly at age 38, leaving his wife, a five year-old daughter, and infant son, Charlie. Nonetheless, from an early age, he regularly regaled friends and relatives with jokes and stories, many of his own creation. As he grew older, Leuchter not surprisingly discussed his desire for a future in theatre. In fact, he would major in theater at the University of Denver, which he attended specifically for that program.

As graduation neared, Charlie anticipated getting drafted, so he preemptively joined the Air Force, hoping for an assignment in an entertainment division. Instead, he found himself being trained as a radar navigator. Leuchter excelled at his new craft. As a result of new technology, practice bombing runs did not actually involve dropping ordnance on the training target. Rather, the radar navigator would "drop a bomb" by triggering a radar beam from the plane, which was aimed at the "target." Mobile ground-based receiving equipment would detect the beam and determine the accuracy of the "bomb drop." A direct hit was referred to as a "shack," recalling an earlier era when the practice targets were actually wooden shanties. Direct hits were difficult to accomplish and did not occur very frequently. Some radar navigators never achieved even one "shack." To his credit, Charlie had scored several "shacks."

Lt. Col. Ken Snyder, USAF (ret.), a standardization crewmate of Leuchter recalled, "Charlie had not changed over the years. He was still a character, an actor, fun to be around…always the entertainer." Both Snyder and Adler shared the following story, characteristic of Leuchter. While on alert one morning, Charlie and his crew arrived in the "mole hole" mess hall for breakfast. Spotting a mop leaning up against a corner wall, he ran over, grabbed the mop, placed it on his head, and to the delight of all, proceeded to parade around the room in the role of *grand dame*. He and his wife, Georgia Jean, were the parents of a daughter, Rachelle "Shelley," and son, David. Charlie had been a senior navigator since May 15, 1962 and had 2824 hours of flight time to his credit.

Captain Charles Leuchter

Joseph R. Wax

3

Heavenward

On January 23, Bulli and Morrison completed and filed the required preflight paperwork for the next day's mission, and Bulli held a briefing with the entire crew in the 99th Bomb Wing standardization offices. They reviewed the flight plan, which included two possible training routes, referred to as "Poker Deck" routes over the continental United States. These routes were developed and published in early November 1962 by the Eighth Air Force specifically for ACR training. The low-level flight paths would expose crews to a variety of terrain contours, while avoiding heavily populated areas and minimizing encounters with other military and civilian air traffic.

The first option was Poker Deck 8-3, where upon reaching the designated radio beacon called the vertical omni range, or VOR, located over the far eastern Maine town of Princeton, the bomber would descend from its cruising altitude to the penetration altitude of five hundred feet above the terrain. The training course then traversed the heavily wooded and sparsely populated northern tier of the state from east to west, passing just south of the town of Millinocket and nearby Mount Katahdin, the northern terminus of the Appalachian Trail. The path continued just north of Moosehead Lake, the largest mountain lake east of the Mississippi, and just north of Greenville, the gateway to the Maine North Woods and a hub for the state's lumber industry. The flight would then loop back east, regaining altitude over the expansive Baxter State Park, and head back to the Princeton VOR before descending and entering another training run.

The second option, Poker Deck 8-5, called for 0406 to head south, descending to penetration altitude at the Chesterfield, South Carolina VOR and flying north-northwest, first in the vicinity of High Point, then Thomasville, Winston-Salem, and Mount Airy in central North Carolina. The aircraft would then bank to the southwest, skirting Asheville to the north, and cruising over the state's "High Country" or Appalachians, which bordered eastern Tennessee and the Great Smoky Mountains National Park. The flight would then climb and head east, looping back to the Chesterfield VOR for its next training run.

Takeoff was initially scheduled for 0800 the following morning, with the final decision regarding route selection to be made based on the respective weather conditions present at the time of the preflight briefing. The flight would be referred to by the call sign "Frosh 10." The crew was expected to be ready at base operations two hours before departure for a final briefing and to allow sufficient time for preflight checks.

Early in the morning hours of January 24, the phone rang at the Bulli household in South Hadley, Massachusetts, informing the aircraft commander that the flight would be delayed because of issues with the ACR. He arose, dressed, and quietly left the house at 0700, taking care to gently close the door so as not to awaken his wife, Evelyn, who had just finally fallen asleep at 0500. Ev, a high school English teacher, had spent the last few days at home tending to their eleven year-old son, John, and nine year-old daughter, Marilyn, both of whom were ill and home from school.

An hour earlier, Jerry Adler and Charlie Leuchter had arrived at base operations in the frozen darkness only to be informed that the takeoff was delayed due to maintenance problems with the ACR. They were dismissed and told to return at 0900. Adler returned home, where his wife and two daughters were still sleeping soundly. He soon followed suit. After a quick nap he headed to the door, stopping first to grab a leather pile-lined cap, extra warm gloves, matches, and a flashlight. Despite, or perhaps as a result of their cumulative hours in the B-52 and years flying for the Air Force, there remained some trepidation among the crew regarding that day's mission. Several years later, Capt. Adler looked back and explained, "It was the wing's first flight after previous cancellations due to weather and faulty equipment. The new system and the unusually low altitudes to be flown caused some of us on the crew to wear even warmer clothing and carry more survival gear than normal."

Just three weeks earlier, the Hills had purchased a new car, a Pontiac Bonneville. As Bob prepared to leave the house for Westover and the day's training mission, he offhandedly informed Mildred, who did not drive, that the car was paid off. On the occasion of the fiftieth anniversary of the flight, she recalled to a local newspaper reporter, "I always wondered why he would tell me that. I think he felt something was going to happen. I think he knew his time was up."

Bob Morrison awoke early for the flight and kissed Irene goodbye as he left the house. She was surprised when just a few moments later the door opened again to find Bob inexplicably stepping back inside. In yet another unusual gesture, he gave her another kiss and told her that he loved her, adding, "Take care of the kids for me." And then, as before, he was gone. Years later, his daughter Shari recalled, "I believe he had a premonition that this flight might not end well. He had also taken out a life insurance policy on his life 6-12 months prior…"

At 0900, as ordered, all nine flyers, seven from the two local crews and the two visiting instructors, assembled at Westover base operations. After a final weather update, they stepped outside and into a warmed and waiting blue Air Force van and were driven to the flight line where 0406 awaited. Accompanying the group was Capt. Ken Snyder, S-47's and Morrison's co-pilot. Ken was along to orient Jerry Adler to the operation of the electronic warfare officer's seat that he would be taking instead of his usual navigator's seat, a result of the unusual crew composition. Following an equipment inspection and walk-around by the pilots, the contingent of nine officers ascended the entry ladder and passed through the open hatch in the belly of the fuselage.

The front crew compartment quickly grew even more cramped than usual, with the addition of the two New Mexico-based instructors. "Upstairs," Bulli harnessed himself into the left front pilot seat, while Morrison settled into the right front co-pilot seat. Just between and behind them, Simpson took the instructor pilot spot. Leuchter sat immediately behind and "back to back" with Simpson. Further behind them, Adler buckled into the electronic warfare officer's station. After running Adler through the seat's operation, Snyder exited the plane and returned to the Base Operations center with the van. Above, only the pilot, co-pilot and EWO seats were equipped to eject. "Downstairs," in the lower aspect of the front crew compartment, Hill took the radar navigator seat on the left and Hanson harnessed himself into the navigator's spot on the right, while Gabriel sat just forward of the front wheel well in the instructor navigator's position. Below, only the radar navigator and navigator seats had ejection mechanisms.

TSgt. O'Keefe climbed up a maintenance ladder that was placed at the rear of the aircraft for him, and he boarded through the small open hatch that accessed the even more cramped tail gunner's compartment. Once on board, he wriggled forward and over his seat back, which had been reclined flat, enabling him to climb over and into the compartment. Once in place, he turned and reached over his shoulder, grasping the seat back and rotating it forward into the upright position. O'Keefe then buckled into his harness, completed his preflight checks and settled in for takeoff.

At 1048, Frosh 10 received clearance to proceed along the planned southern route, but 12 minutes later, the flight crew again had to delay their preflight routine for additional radar maintenance. During the delay, another weather update was requested from the base weather station, referred to by "Westover Metro."

Frosh one zero	"Frosh one zero, Westover Metro, this is Frosh one zero"
Metro	"One zero, Westover Metro."
Frosh one zero	"Roger Metro. How does that northern poker deck route look now?
Metro	"Stand by one."
Frosh one zero	"Roger"
Metro	"One zero, Westover Metro. Last report shows most of the cloudiness as (garbled) as over the hills. Weather report from Greenville, Maine and the last report shows some broken clouds about three thousand feet over the mountain tops and out over the flatlands and marshes. Scattered decks about three thousand feet just as about what I told you before. I'm sure I told you I had broken clouds around the hilltops. Otherwise it will be scattered in VFR, over."
Frosh one zero	"Ah, Roger. I think we'll go south."

Metro   "Roger"

At 1135, Bulli radioed base operations, requesting clearance for takeoff and permission to fly over the local area where the ACR could be calibrated before embarking on the training portion of the mission. Permission was granted, preflight preparations were completed, and at 1157 Frosh 10 reported that it was ready for takeoff. Final clearance and flight plan approval came at 1159. Bulli started an inboard engine, from which billowed a cloud of white exhaust smoke as it ignited. Once it had warmed up, he lit the remaining engines as the ground crew removed the plane's connections to its portable auxiliary power units. The massive bomber slowly taxied to the end of the 11,597 foot-long runway 23. The brakes were released and he eased the eight lollipop-stick throttle controls forward, each of the eight whining Pratt and Whitney engines unleashing over 12,000 pounds of thrust as the plane barreled ahead, accelerating steadily. Trailing characteristic streams of thick black exhaust, Frosh 10 finally lifted off, becoming airborne at 1211, more than four hours behind schedule.

Aided by Maj. Gabriel, Hanson and Hill were dealing with the ornery ACR system. Based on the aircraft's altimeter readings, they knew their actual altitude as well as the altitude relative to the terrain features over which they passed. The ACR readings, however, were incorrect. At 1222, Frosh 10 radioed Westover, informing base operations of the issue, and the crew's intention to remain in the local air space until it was resolved. Three minutes later, the crew requested ground assistance in working through the glitch.

Bulli and Morrison flew in the area of nearby Holyoke, Massachusetts and Mount Tom, a 1200-foot peak of craggy volcanic rock ringed with cliffs and the tallest peak of the Metacomet Ridge of the Mount Tom Range. Mount Tom shared a tragic history with Westover Air Force Base. On the rainy night of July 9, 1946, a B-17 Flying Fortress bomber, converted for postwar military transport duty, was on final approach to Westover when it crashed into the local landmark, three hundred feet below the summit. All twenty-five servicemen aboard perished.

On the lower deck, the problem with the ACR became clear by 1330. The radar was providing an altitude reading that was exactly 300 feet higher than actual. In other words, if the actual altitude was 500 feet, the plane's altimeter read 500 feet, but the ACR reported the altitude as 800 feet. All efforts were unable to eliminate this erroneous but consistent discrepancy. Regardless, as the glitch was consistent and predictable, the navigators and pilots could easily compensate with straightforward altitude reading corrections. The mission would proceed.

On the upper deck, following the multiple delays, the pilots were reconsidering the original plan to fly the southern route. That mission would have taken 6 hours 45 minutes from takeoff to landing, while the northern route was of shorter duration, requiring 5 hours 30 minutes. The mission's goals were to provide each three-person team of pilot, navigator, and radar navigator two training "runs" through the designated training course, for a total of four runs during that day's flight. Each run through the northern route was calculated to take 32.5 minutes in windless conditions, and would be followed by a 15 minute return flight to the next run's starting point, for a total time of 47.5 minutes from the beginning to the end of each cycle. Weather conditions permitting, electing the northern route at this point would allow completion of the assignment and return to Westover in approximately 4.5 hours. Frosh 10 now radioed Westover Metro for an updated weather briefing on the northern poker deck route.

Frosh one zero	"Westover Metro, this is Frosh 10"
Metro	"Aircraft calling Westover Metro, this is Westover Metro. Go ahead."
Frosh one zero	" Roger, this is Frosh 10 and we are still in the local area here, will you give me a reading on the northern poker deck area at the present time? Is that improving any up there?"
Metro	"Roger 10, this is Westover Metro, stand by while I check the very latest on that. Roger stand by."
Metro	"Westover, this is Westover Metro, Poker Deck generally scattered in the flatlands still looks like however, it will be scattered to broken with bases from around 2,000 to 2,500 in the south, in the hills, with tops around 6,500MSI. Also received a report, expect anyway, moderate turbulence, with occasionally severe turbulence in some of the

hills. We do not have Mt. Washington to the
south, it is still zero, zero, fog, and blowing
snow. And we also have a report on
Greenville, showing that it is scattered, the
restricted visibility is down, and blowing
snow. But the general condition at Greenville
is 2500 scattered and ten. It looks like the flat
country will be scattered, occasionally broken
in the hills and some of the hills obscured,
over. Ten, this is Metro. Did you read? Over."

Frosh one zero — "Roger, 10 here. Be advised you are coming
in, your transmissions are very, very garbled
and chewed up, and hard to read."

Metro — 10, Westover Metro, 10 Westover Metro, how
do you read me now?"

Frosh one zero — "You're coming in better now, Metro."

Metro — "This is Westover Metro. I repeat, the
flatlands in the northern poker deck route is
generally high thin scattered clouds, bases
around 2500 feet, tops about 5000. In the
higher terrain you can expect 2500 scattered
to broken with a few isolated snow showers,
that is MSL on the 2500 feet. Tops about
6000 still expect moderate turbulence change
to occasionally severe turbulence in the hills.

We have a report from Mt. Washington to the south of your route. It shows they are still zero, zero, and fog and blowing snow. Over. 10, this is Westover Metro. Did you read me that time? Over."

Frosh one zero

"Thank you very much, Metro. This is Frosh 10 out."

Bulli and Morrison considered the latest transmission from Metro. The preflight briefing for the local Westover vicinity had noted winds of 15 miles per hour with gusts to 25 miles per hour and moderate turbulence from the surface to an altitude of 6000 feet. However, Frosh 10 had not encountered any turbulence since takeoff, leading them to question not just the accuracy of the original weather report, but now the latest one, as well. Bulli subsequently recalled, "Because of the fact that the forecaster had missed the forecast on turbulence at Westover so badly, we felt that he was probably off on this area, too. So we presumed since the surface winds were comparable within such a short span there, that it would be relatively the same up north. And, in fact, it was." The time was 1341. Navigator Capt. Herb Hanson set the course and Frosh 10 headed north to Maine and Poker Deck 8-3.

Joseph R. Wax

4

Aloft

Aircraft commander Dan Bulli had the controls and eased the plane up, reaching a cruising altitude of 27,000 feet at 1351. 0406 continued to the northeast, passing over Concord and Augusta, the capitals of New Hampshire and Maine, until it reached the Princeton VOR at 1420. Frosh 10 requested and received clearance to fly within 100 nautical miles of the Princeton VOR for a two-hour window under visual flight rules. Bulli nudged the control column forward, causing the plane to descend at four thousand feet per minute. At 1431, the penetration altitude of 500 feet was achieved and Frosh 10 entered low-level flight for its initial ACR training run. Senior radar navigator Maj. Bob Hill provided the course readings to Bulli under the guidance of the instructor master navigator Maj. William Gabriel.

Cruising through clear blue skies with unlimited visibility, scattered clouds, and just occasional pockets of mild turbulence seemed to confirm Bulli's interpretation of the weather forecasts, the actual conditions aloft, and the decision to fly the northern route. An unpredictable and unforeseen confluence of events, however, would abruptly change that assessment.

Turbulence simply refers to disrupted or irregular air movement resulting from changing air currents. It is further described by its effects on aircraft as light, moderate, severe, or extreme. Light turbulence is associated with slight, momentary erratic changes in altitude or attitude of the plane. One might feel some strain against the seatbelt and unsecured objects might be moved about. Walking about the cabin remains possible, though is not recommended. Moderate turbulence is characterized by greater changes in altitude or attitude. One definitely strains against the seatbelt and unsecured items are dislodged. Walking about the cabin is difficult and should not be attempted. The pilot remains in positive control of the aircraft at all times. Severe turbulence results in large, abrupt changes in altitude or attitude and one will be forced violently against the seatbelt. Unsecured items will be thrown about the cabin. Standing and walking are impossible, and the pilot may momentarily lose control of the aircraft. In extreme turbulence, the plane is tossed about violently and essentially impossible to control. Structural damage to the aircraft can occur.

Turbulence may further be categorized by its cause as frontal, wind shear, thermal, or mechanical in origin. Frontal turbulence happens when the sloping edges of cold air and warm air masses meet, forming a front. The warm air then rises along the sloping edge of the cold air, causing friction between the two air masses, which produces turbulence. Wind shear turbulence occurs when winds quickly change horizontal or vertical speed and direction over a very short distance. Thermal, or convective, turbulence occurs when the earth's surface air becomes warmed and rises into the atmosphere, while the higher, cooler air descends through the atmosphere. The currents created by this cycle cause the plane to rise and fall, resulting in the bumpy ride felt on board a plane flying through the turbulence.

Mechanical turbulence occurs near the ground when winds flow against and over man-made or natural objects such as buildings or mountains. Imagine the wind as being analogous to a flowing river. Next, picture the river flowing downstream against and around a large boulder in the center of the river. Small circular swirling currents called eddys develop on the downstream side of the boulder as a result of the disrupted water current. What happens when wind flows against and over large irregular terrain structures? As the "upstream" or windward airflow meets and passes over the building or mountain, the friction generated by the air's contact with the structure and the ground causes eddys, also referred to as rotors, to develop in the air on the "downstream" or lee side of the object. These rotors are a source of potentially severe turbulence.

Another turbulence-inducing phenomenon that results from the interaction of winds with mountains is referred to as mountain or lee waves. Mountain waves are created when strong winds flowing perpendicular to the mountain ridge pass up and over the mountain and encounter a stable air mass. Unable to penetrate the stable air mass above, the winds are initially deflected downward toward the earth's surface. The winds, however, do not reach the surface as they are deflected again, this time upward by a second and lower stable air mass. The winds again encounter the upper stable air mass, reinitiating this cycle, resulting in an up and down, or sinusoidal, wind pattern that can extend for miles. Mountain waves generally result in undulating but smooth airflow, but updrafts and downdrafts within the wave can cause violent turbulence. Turbulence also can also occur if the waves "break" and disrupt airflow, just as a tall wave in the ocean crests and breaks as it approaches the shore. Finally, lee waves may generate rotors below the peak of the mountain, which, as noted, cause severe turbulence.

The bomber continued along its selected training route, maintaining its prescribed altitude of 500 feet above the terrain at a speed of 280 knots. It screamed over the treetops in the hamlet of Brownville, Maine. Selectman Vernald Larson was chatting with Mrs. Rowena Porter, the town clerk, in the municipal building, when 0406 roared past. The pair ran to a nearby window and witnessed the spectacle of the massive low-flying aircraft trailing its streams of black engine exhaust, thinking that it was almost close enough to touch.

At the same time, Brownville resident Mrs. Freda Melanson had just backed out of her driveway onto Route 11 and headed northeast on her way to neighboring Brownville Junction. She marveled at the plane as it flew directly overhead, then onward, seemingly following the path of the highway. The jet then banked to the left, heading northwest and beyond Mrs.

Melanson's view as she continued along Route 11 in the opposite direction, with her husband at her side.

Twelve miles away at Silver Lake, Robert Emery, an employee of the timber logging concern Prentiss and Carlisle Company, Inc., was atop a Caterpillar road grader, plowing 18 inches of freshly fallen snow near the long-since abandoned Katahdin Iron Works ore mine. As 0406 passed overhead, Emery, like the three other local folks just seconds before, could not help but stare at the flight's progress. He watched the huge jet fly west over Chairback Mountain and out of sight.

The navigator during the first terrain avoidance advanced capability radar training run, Capt. Herb Hanson, notified the pilots over the interphone, or on board intercom, that the plane would soon reach the next designated turn along its flight path, setting a course back east and to the start of the second training run. Previously, at several points along the low level portion of the flight, the instructor pilot, Lt. Col. Simpson, had directed Bulli to fly slightly off course, never by more than two to three miles and still in accordance with the prescribed flight path, to take advantage of the varying terrain features, observing and learning their different presentations on the radar scope. Now, Simpson postponed the impending turn and directed the crew to continue on its current course, intending to fly over an upcoming mountain three miles distant to the northwest, and gain experience with the terrain avoidance radar's graphic presentation of its contour.

The target was Elephant Mountain, a 2647-foot peak with a ridgeline running from the southwest to the northeast. Unknown to the crew of 0406,

40-knot gusting winds from the northwest were whipping off of Moosehead Lake on a near-perpendicular course to the windward western slope of the mountain. Up and over the ridgeline flowed the icy currents, creating turbulence–inducing mountain waves, which propagated over and beyond the leeward eastern slope. The aircraft continued on its northwesterly and nearly perpendicular approach to the leeward eastern side of Elephant Mountain's ridgeline, headed directly toward the unseen, yet powerfully churning waves of air.

The western slope of Elephant Mountain viewed from nearby Lower Wilson Pond. (Photo by the author)

5

Earthward

As the bomber approached Elephant Mountain, the turbulence felt on board increased, and 0406 was quickly hammered by two hard jolts. Co-pilot Maj. Bob Morrison maintained the plane steady at the prescribed air speed of 280 knots. Several seconds and half a mile later, the aircraft was pounded by increasingly severe bursts of turbulence. Bulli announced that they were "going up" to a higher altitude to escape the turbulence and seek smoother air, exactly the maneuver prescribed under the circumstances. Simpson agreed. Bulli switched from flying by the advanced capability terrain avoidance radar to the more familiar standard instruments. He eased the nose up five degrees while maintaining the air speed at 280 knots. Severe turbulence continued to pummel 0406.

Immediately there was what sounded like a loud sharp explosion from the aft right side of the plane. The aircraft instantly pitched nose down five degrees and banked 40 degrees to the right. Bulli tried to correct the plane's attitude with full left rudder, full left aileron, and nose up trim. Despite his efforts, the airspeed accelerated to 300 knots and the plane remained nose down in a descending right turn. All instruments appeared to be functioning normally, though the plane was vibrating so severely that Bulli could barely read them. He moved Morrison's hands off the throttles and slowed the four port, or left-sided, engines. There was no response to Bulli's maneuvers. What he did not know was that there had been no explosion. Worse, and unknown at that moment to all on board, the thirty foot tall vertical stabilizer, or upright tail fin, which was responsible for keeping the plane flying straight, had broken free and been completely avulsed from the fuselage by the turbulence. All efforts to control the direction of flight were futile. 0406 continued along its lethal path toward the ground.

Capt. Jerry Adler, the second navigator on board as part of the hybrid training crew, was still sitting in the electronic warfare officer's position behind the pilots on the upper level of the crew compartment, awaiting his turn for the next training run when the loud blast racked the plane. As 0406 headed down and banked right, he was tossed to the right in his seat, his harness snapping taught against him. As his body strained against the straps, looking through a window that normally would have been beyond his line of sight, he could see the tree tops racing past at what appeared to be just arm's reach away. Fear struck as he realized 0406's impending fate. Time slowed to a crawl. He could only hang on and wait for the order to abandon the aircraft.

The vertical stabilizer from 0406 still remains where it landed at the base of the eastern slope of Elephant Mountain. The fin's top is to the photo's left, while the avulsed base is to the right. (Photo by the author)

"Bail out, bail out!," Bulli ordered over the interphone. However, he could not hear himself speaking and changed the on board communication switch position, again ordering the crew to "Bail out, bail out!" He then flipped on the bail out alarm bell and lights, providing two additional warnings to the crew to abandon the plane.

Remarkably, after nearly 60 years of exposure to the elements, the aircraft's tail number 0406 is still visible on the vertical stabilizer. (Photo by the author)

Adler also did not hear Bulli's call over the interphone to bail out. His clear blue eyes turned expectantly to the abandon light – it was now glowing a steady red, signaling the crew to evacuate the aircraft. He fought against the forces that continued pressing him against the right side of his seat to reach the left armrest's arming lever, rotating it upward and locking himself into his seat in preparation for ejection while blowing off the overhead escape hatch. As he prepared to continue the ejection sequence, a rush of frigid air poured into the crew's compartment through the opening left by the jettisoned escape hatch, sending the papers from his desk swirling through the cabin. He then grasped the right armrest's ejection arming lever, and rotated it upward, feeling the seat drop down and rearward. With the crippled plane 100 feet above the ground and skimming the treetops, the fingers of Adler's right hand gripped the ejection trigger and squeezed.

The explosive charge underneath detonated, firing him and his seat upward and off of its rails, rocketing him out the top of the fuselage through the opening left by his now-jettisoned escape hatch. As he shot upward, a bizarre thought entered Adler's mind. "So this is what it is like to eject," he pondered. He was the first man to bail out of the stricken plane.

Capt. Jerry Adler's ejection seat on display at the Center for Moosehead History's Moosehead Lake Aviation Museum, Greenville, Maine. (Photo by the author)

This was Adler's first flight in which he was seated on the upper deck of the B-52 in one of the three upward-ejecting crew seats located there, those of the pilot, co-pilot, and electronic warfare officer. As a B-52 navigator for over four years, Adler had always flown in the "downstairs" navigator's seat, located in the lower crew compartment, along with that of the radar navigator. In contrast to the upper deck seats, during ejection the navigator and radar navigator seats would be shot downward through escape hatches in the bottom of the fuselage. The downward ejection was initiated by the crew-member first rotating an arming lever upward, then grasping a large triggering ring located between his legs and pulling upward. As the lower-seat occupant was ejected from the plane, a separation harness would pull taught under the flier, and effectively throw the individual out of the seat automatically and trigger his parachute to deploy. Adler was, not surprisingly, well acquainted with this system. During pre-flight preparations, however, he learned that at the start of the mission he would be occupying the "upstairs" electronic warfare officer's position while awaiting his turn on the ACR. However, unlike the downward ejection's mechanism of automatically separating flier from seat with parachute deployment, upward ejection required the flier to kick forward after exiting the aircraft to activate separation from the seat and deploy one's parachute. Fortunately, Ken Snyder had reviewed the ejection procedure with Adler just prior to takeoff. Unfortunately, Adler reflexively fell back on his ingrained training after departing 0406 - he did not kick forward.

Co-pilot Bob Morrison was the second to heed the abandon order, immediately ejecting successfully and deploying his parachute as he was separated from his seat. Just ten seconds had passed since 0406 lost its vertical stabilizer and Bulli lost control of 0406.

Maj. Bob Morrison's ejection seat on display at the Maine Air Museum, Bangor, Maine. The museum is located on the grounds of Bangor International Airport, formerly Dow Air Force Base (Photo by the author)

In the far aft tail gunner's compartment, the initial explosion was deafening to Mike O'Keefe. Even though he was buckled into his seat harness, he was violently snapped about his cramped quarters by the plane's erratic motion. Facing rearward as 0406 flew nose-down while banking to the right, the tree tops raced past an arms length away while the crystal blue winter sky dotted with a few thin scattered clouds filled his view to the right. On the order to bail out, standard operating procedure was for the tail gunner to pull the yellow lever that would engage the mechanism that jettisoned his glass turret dome and gun housing, opening his compartment to the sky, into which he was expected to roll out of the plane's rear with his parachute and escape. In order to prevent an inadvertent jettison should the tail gunner accidently activate the release, the turret release was equipped with a 30 second delay. With the bail out light on, O'Keefe pulled the lever and waited.

Adler's parachute never deployed. He remained harnessed in his seat, which represented his only remaining connection to the aircraft, tumbling head over heels while clutching the armrests "for dear life" as "there was nothing else to hold on to," and hurtling toward the ground. Man and seat crashed through the forest canopy, snapping heavy limbs from trees, drilling through the five foot deep snow pack, and impacting the ground with a force later estimated as equivalent to sixteen times gravity. Adler landed upright, chest high in snow, still harnessed to his seat, unconscious, yet somehow alive. His injuries were later catalogued to include fractures of the skull and the right third, fourth, and fifth ribs. Unbeknown to anyone, including himself, in that instant Capt. Gerald J. Adler, USAF became the first and only human to eject in a Weber Aircraft ejection seat or eject from an airborne B-52 and survive without the parachute deploying. Unbeknown to Capt. Adler, his ordeal was just beginning.

Bulli continued to struggle at the controls of 0406, trying to remain airborne as long as he could to give the remaining crew time to eject. Visibility through the cockpit windows was obscured by the maelstrom of papers and debris launched first by Adler's and then by Morrison's departure. Visibility was, however, sufficiently good for Bulli to see that the aircraft was headed directly for the snow-covered rock-strewn summit of Elephant Mountain. Twenty seconds had elapsed since he was last in control of 0406.

No time remained to for Bulli to initiate the complete recommended ejection procedure of lowering his helmet visor to prevent eye injury, actuating a bail out bottle providing oxygen to breathe, or raising and squeezing the left armrest lever that would stow the vertical control column fully forward so that he could eject without striking it, and set off a charge to blow open his overhead escape hatch. Bulli could only manage to execute the final step of the ejection sequence, raising the right armrest handle, squeezing the trigger lever, and firing the explosive charge that launched him in his seat. As he shot upward, his left foot and ankle were shattered upon impacting the control column, which had not been stowed. His helmet and seat back were slammed against the unopened overhead escape hatch, blasting it free of the fuselage, and sending both man and seat skyward. He felt his parachute open.

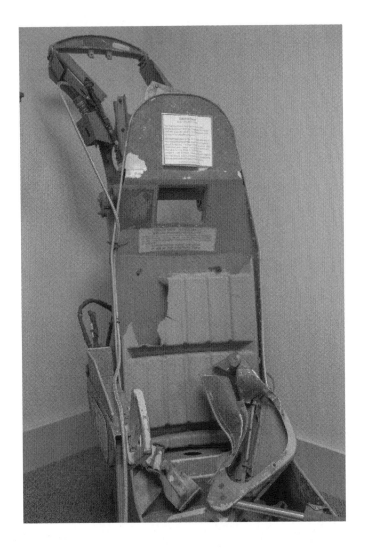

Lt. Col. Dan Bulli's ejection seat on display at the Center for Moosehead History's Moosehead Lake Aviation Museum, Greenville, Maine. Discovered in the woods in 2012, the top of the seat back was crushed during ejection as it slammed into the unopened escape hatch. (Photo by the author)

Navigator Herb Hanson and radar navigator Bob Hill were at their stations in the lower crew compartment for the initial ACR training run. The pair was buckled into their downward ejecting seats when the bailout signals were activated. Next to them were instructor navigator William Gabriel and the second Westover radar navigator, Charlie Leuchter, who was observing the equipment's operation while standing by for his training run with navigator Jerry Adler. Gabriel's and Leuchter's seats were not equipped with ejection mechanisms. Crew occupying these two locations were expected to bail out by hurling themselves out the openings left in the bottom of the fuselage following the downward ejections of the nearby navigators. This same plan applied to the person seated in the non-ejecting instructor pilot seat, who additionally would first have to climb down the ladder linking the upper and lower crew compartments before departing. Designed for high altitude egress, successful downward ejection required the aircraft to be at a minimum altitude of 400 feet to allow sufficient time and space for parachute deployment and slowing the speed of the flier's descent. 0406 had already descended below 300 feet and continued to plummet.

The massive bomber flew onward, barely clearing the ridgeline, and dropping from view as the mountain's western slope fell away. The plane's right wing tip knifed through the snow pack and into the frozen ground, shearing the entire structure from the fuselage. Jet fuel poured from the wing's shredded fuel tanks, instantly igniting from the sparks generated by the friction of metal on rock and the heat from the four avulsed engines. The left wing suffered the same fate, further fueling the flames that now engulfed nearby trees and brush. The fuselage snowplowed across the forest floor, disintegrating along the three football field-long path that it carved. Acrid black smoke billowed heavenward, marking the flight's final resting place. For personnel used to 24-hour airborne missions, this flight should have been, as Capt. Adler would describe, "as easy as a trip to the grocery store." It had been just that - up until 30 seconds earlier.

The wind carried Bulli along at an estimated 50 miles per hour, as he, too, just barely skimmed over the top of the mountain's ridge. To his left, he saw the flaming remains of 0406, although he never heard the impact or the following explosion. To his right, he saw another open orange chute, belonging to Bob Morrison, being carried along a parallel path eastward, away from the crash site and toward thickly forested terrain. As Bulli wondered whether he would drift into the roiling crucible below, an updraft created by the heat from the flaming wreckage swept him another estimated 1000 feet up into the air. Airborne debris swirled about him. His helmet visor was still up as he sailed down toward the forested landscape. He reflexively raised his arms protectively to cover his eyes and face. Knowing that his left leg was injured, Bulli drew up his right leg to cushion the impact as he crashed into the trees broadside with his right side leading.

6

Search, Rescue, Recovery

Shortly after the bomber disappeared from view behind Chairback Mountain, the heavy equipment operator, Robert Emery, saw a huge cloud of black smoke rising above the mountain ridge, four miles distant. He could not hear an explosion over the rumbling of the diesel running beneath him. Emery grabbed his radio and reported what he just saw to John Ferguson back at the Prentiss and Carlisle Company office. John Ferguson then picked up his telephone and called the Maine State Police, which in turn called the Base Command Post at Dow Air Force Base in Bangor, Maine some 50 miles distant. At 1516, the crash phone rang at the Dow Base Fire Department with the news that a B-52C based out of Westover had crashed. The search for the plane and its crew had begun. Just 24 minutes had elapsed since 0406 fell from the sky.

The Air Force, Maine Air National Guard, Maine Warden Service, Maine State Police, Civil Air Patrol, and local businesses and civilians quickly joined the search and rescue efforts. A helicopter based at Dow quickly arrived on scene, passing over the area where the plane was believed to have gone down without spotting any parachutes or signs of the wreckage. Maine Warden Pilot Andrew Stinson flying his single engine plane also searched unsuccessfully. As the sun began to set, rescue personnel converged on tiny Brownville Junction.

The search headquarters was established at the local Canadian Pacific railroad station. Maj. J.W. Henderson took the lead. Two ground search teams of between thirty and thirty-five men arrived that evening from Dow, commanded by Capt. James R. "Russ" McCarthy, Director of Safety at the base. As darkness fell, ground search efforts were suspended until morning. Later that evening, the crew of a Dow-based KC-97, a four-engine propeller–driven tanker based on the B-29 bomber, flew over the suspected crash area and spotted two fires believed to be from a burning aircraft and radioed their position. Further search efforts would have to wait until dawn.

Cots and bunks were set up throughout the command post building, now a makeshift barracks, for the airmen to quarter until they were dispatched into the steep snow-covered terrain the following morning. Snow removal and rescue equipment and vehicles were brought in. However, subfreezing temperatures prevented vehicles' engines from starting. Ether and dry gas helped resolve this issue. However, once running, vehicles either slid off the icy roads or refused to climb the slippery hilly ground. More gear and men moved the effort forward.

Earlan Campbell and his son, Wayne, along with friend Robert "Bob" Hume, of Millinocket, Maine produced three Sno-Travelers, precursors of today's snowmobiles, to help access the search area, which was buried in five feet of snow, with drifts up to 15 feet deep. Earlan had opened the first snowmobile dealership in Maine just five years earlier, and worked closely with Polaris Industries to design and trial their early prototypes in the far reaches of northern Maine. He would eventually become the first Mainer inducted into the Snowmobile Hall of Fame in St. Germain, Wisconsin.

Henderson spent a sleepless night in the stationmaster's office, poring over maps for possible routes into the vicinity and preparing for the next day's rescue. John Bishop, a heavy equipment operator for the railroad was called in from his LaGrange, Maine home to clear a football field-sized helicopter landing area. He, too, spent a sleepless night, finishing his assigned task as the first chopper approached shortly after daybreak. Maine guide, Arthur Ogden, of Brownville Junction, appeared and offered his services. Henry Graves, owner of a local filling station, placed himself on call throughout the night for personnel in need of fuel. The local grocery and variety store followed suit, remaining open to provision the search and rescuers.

After an unknown interval, Adler regained consciousness, hearing nothing but overwhelming silence. Surrounded by trees, snow, and stillness, he saw smoke from the crash site rising in the distance. He struggled to get up, finally managing to reach the snow-covered buckles restraining his legs, first releasing them and then himself. Looking around, he saw that the parachute was still on his back where it belonged and that only the small two-foot diameter pilot chute had deployed. Adler, carrying the parachute pack, struck off in the direction of a frozen water body visible from his vantage point, planning to open and spread out the orange-colored main parachute on the lake's icy surface as a signal to rescuers. The snow, though, was shoulder deep and quickly soaked his boots and flight suit.

As the leaves had fallen off the trees months earlier, he decided his current location would be visible from the air and instead opted to remain in place. He spread the chute for a signal and attempted to light a fire with the matches he had placed in his pocket barely six hours earlier as an afterthought on the way out of his home. He efforts were for naught– the available tinder was just too wet to catch. He shouted, but the only reply was continued silence. Adler next tried to remove the standard issue survival kit from its container housed in the bottom of his ejection seat. He grasped at it, but it wouldn't budge. The force of his landing had driven the seat bottom to the ground, bending the metal housing around the kit, which was now stubbornly locked in it's vise-like grip. Using the two knives he carried, Adler then attempted to first pry open, then cut into the kit to access its contents. His efforts proved fruitless.

Dusk approached. The smoke that Adler initially saw after crashing to earth was no longer visible. Another unusual thought intruded into his mind, "Maybe I panicked and left a flyable airplane." He wondered whether, after being rescued, on his return he "would be welcomed or court-martialed." Adler gathered his parachute, wrapping himself within its folds, trying to shelter himself from the cold. Nothing happened, no communication with anyone. He knew that the aircraft would not be missed until it failed to radio its hourly position report. He settled in to wait.

When Bulli lowered his arms from his face and looked around, he found himself 30 feet in the air, suspended by his parachute between the trunks of two trees. Finding it difficult to breathe, he pulled off his oxygen mask, which provided no oxygen flow following the incomplete ejection sequence. Breathing was immediately easier. He sat in his harness and took stock of his situation. Bulli tried to pull the quick release for the survival kit from the bottom of his parachute, but it did not fall free- the release was broken. He reached his fingers into a one-inch opening in the retaining zipper, forcing it open. He watched the survival kit plummet to the ground and disappear into the snow. The rubberized life raft, included as survival equipment, also fell and sank three inches into the snow.

Unable to grasp any limbs, and assisted by the increasing wind, he began to swing himself back and forth like a pendulum in increasingly wide arcs, eventually able to grab onto a nearby five-inch thick tree trunk. By now, Bulli's hands were cold and stiff as his thin leather flying gloves provided little protection against the elements. Blood drained from his left glove. He had hit the trees with such force that a branch had punctured his left glove, passed through his index finger, and exited out the other side of the glove. He gripped the branch with his teeth and pulled, extracting the wooden spike from his perforated flesh. Using the sides of his hands, since his fingers were numb, he released himself from his parachute by unlocking the chest and leg straps, and slid down the tree. Bulli found that he was now caught in the crotch of the tree. He extricated himself and fell, joining his gear in five feet of powdery snow.

Bulli attempted to stand, but his injured left leg gave way-it was completely numb. He crawled uphill 15 feet to where the survival kit and raft had dropped. He inflated the raft and flipped it upside down, climbing on top and clearing snow from his boots and flight suit. Bulli dug his survival kit out of the snow, a task made easier since it was attached to the raft by a line. He opened the kit and placed iodine on his punctured left index finger, wrapped it with a compress, and pulled wool socks over both hands for warmth. Bulli took off his helmet to put on a wool facemask, after which he replaced his helmet. He inventoried the survival kit, placing all items that could freeze such as water and food, as well as the radio, flashlight, matches, and signal mirror under his thermal underwear to keep them warm. He opened the sleeping bag, placing one side of its hard plastic container over the raft's side onto the snow. The raft shifted and bumped into the container's cover, promptly puncturing and deflating the raft.

Bulli ate one lump of sugar and crawled into his sleeping bag to warm up and consider his situation. The plastic sleeping bag cover that had irreparably damaged his raft was now made useful as a windbreak around his head. Once again warm and thinking clearly, he rechecked the kit's contents for painkillers, but found none. He climbed out of the sleeping bag and dug an 18-inch deep by seven-foot long trench, which he lined with the deflated raft. He replaced the sleeping bag and survival kit contents on top of the raft, then built a berm to serve as a windbreak along the upwind side of his new quarters. Once more, Bulli inventoried his supplies as darkness fell at 1633 and he settled in for the night.

As night fell, Adler could not know the time, nor did it matter. When he hit the ground, his Bulova navigator wristwatch had stopped at 1452. Glad that he had worn his winter flight suit and added long johns for the flight, Adler was also thankful for having grabbed the pile-lined leather hat, heavy warm gloves, and flashlight along with the matches. He tried to stay awake, fearful of falling asleep, thinking of returning to his wife and two young daughters. Eventually, the cold and shock became too much and he faded into unconsciousness.

Capt. Jerry Adler's Bulova navigator watch, its hands forever frozen on the time of his miraculous landing on January 24, 1963. (Photo courtesy of Karen Adler)

During the night, Adler awoke to the sound of a plane overhead. By its lights, he recognized it as a KC-97 Stratofreighter. He signaled an SOS with his flashlight, hopes buoyed by the thought that he had been spotted when he was bathed in its landing lights. "I'll be out pretty soon," he thought, and relaxed. As Adler would later learn, he was neither spotted nor to be rescued shortly. Once more he fought sleep, yet wracked with pain and exhaustion, nodded off again. While he slept, Adler's left leg and booted foot slipped out of the parachute's folds and gently settled into the soft snow. The air temperature was 30 degrees below zero.

In contrast to other mammals, humans do not possess the physiology necessary for tolerating cold temperatures and coming away from the exposure unscathed. The skin, our largest organ, plays a central role in maintaining a steady body temperature that supports life. When in a hot environment, blood vessels within the skin dilate or open wide, increasing blood flow toward the skin surface, thereby allowing the skin to act as a radiator and dissipate excess heat to the environment.

In the converse scenario, when the ambient temperature drops, the initial response is vasoconstriction- a reflex narrowing of the tiny veins and arteries within the skin, reducing blood flow to the surface and redirecting flow to the life- sustaining core organs-the heart, lungs, brain, kidneys, and gut-thereby conserving precious heat and maintaining bodily functions. The diversion of blood in this manner primarily affects the extremities – fingers, hands, toes, and feet-as well as the ears and nose.

As the temperature continues to plummet below freezing, the connections between the individual cells that form the lining of the skin's blood vessels break, much like cracks forming in the mortar of a brick wall. Water from within cells leaks out through the cracks, and tracks into the skin itself causing swelling-a condition referred to as edema. Normally, a cell's shape and function is maintained by its own internal water content, just as a child's bouncy house depends on pumped in air to remain inflated. Turn off the air pump and the bouncy house collapses. When water leaks out of a cell, the cell collapses, function ceases, and the cell dies. Additionally, as the cells collapse and rupture, several chemicals are released that cause blood clots to form within the microscopic skin vessels, cutting off the already reduced blood flow, delivery of oxygen and vital nutrients, and causing death of the involved tissue, referred to as gangrene.

In addition to these life-threatening changes, ongoing exposure to subfreezing cold temperatures can cause injury by yet another mechanism. The water remaining within cells, as well as the water leaked from cells, can completely freeze into ice crystals. As every schoolchild is taught, when water freezes it expands. Ice crystals that form within a cell will cause the cell to expand and eventually rupture, with the same end result as if it had collapsed. Regardless of the causative mechanism of cold-induced tissue death, this phenomenon is colloquially referred to as frostbite.

A variety of other factors can increase the chance of developing frostbite beyond the risks conferred by weather conditions alone. Adler was experiencing many of these factors including dehydration, overexertion, trauma, wet clothing, inadequate insulation, immobility, physical and mental stress, and a long duration of exposure to cold. Scientific tables published by the National Weather Service describe the length of exposure required to induce frostbite at various combinations of air temperature and wind. The conditions on Elephant Mountain at the time Jerry Adler's left leg slipped out of the cocooning folds of his parachute were expected to cause frostbite in less than 30 minutes.

Bulli, too, heard and saw a helicopter, a KC-135 (a military tanker used for in-air refueling operation which was based on an airframe similar to that of the Boeing 707 civilian airliner), and the same KC-97 upon which Jerry Adler had misplaced his rescue hopes. All three aircraft flew directly overhead several times, and like Adler, Bulli found himself illuminated in daylight conditions created by the KC-97's landing lights. Also like Adler, Bulli remained invisible to the crew of the KC-97. He attempted to radio the rescue aircraft unsuccessfully, hearing only static in return to his calls. No voice contact was possible. Similar to Adler's efforts, he tried to attract attention using a combination of his flashlight and mirror, again to no avail. Bulli next tried to walk to a pine tree located 40 feet away, which he planned to set on fire as a distress signal, but his damaged left leg again caused him to collapse in pain. He crawled back to the trench, brushed off the snow, and climbed back into his sleeping bag.

He filled a plastic canteen with snow, tucking it in the sleeping bag next to him, anticipating that heat from his body would melt the snow and provide drinking water. His efforts only produced one-half cup of water. Though thirsty, he did not want to open his survival kit's can of water so as to conserve his rations. Nor did he want to eat snow as a water source for fear of further lowering his body temperature. Bulli placed the instruction book from his survival kit under his hip for insulation as he lay sleeping. He also decided to not eat any food rations until the next morning in case he wasn't picked up for several days.

By now, Bulli thought, the crash area had probably been pinpointed and rescue could reasonably be expected the following day if the weather held. However, little sleep was to be had. He was tormented wondering about the fate of his crew and what caused the plane to crash. He worried about his wife, Evelyn, and two children, John and Marilyn, knowing that once they were notified that he was missing, they, too, would share a long night. It was difficult to nod off for any extended period of time, much less at all, with the constant pain from his left foot and ankle. The wind picked up and he could hear his parachute being blown about and dragged through the trees. He became concerned that it would be swept away from his location, misdirecting rescuers, further delaying being found, or worse yet, not be seen at all by airborne searchers. Some time around 0300, the sky became overcast and sleet began to fall, finally stopping over an hour later. The skies then cleared, along with Bulli's spirits. At dawn, he ate a second sugar cube. Without leaving his sleeping bag, Bulli gathered as many twigs as he could to use as kindling to light a signal fire. He sliced strips of rubber from the flaps on the raft to feed the nascent flames and waited.

Life-threatening stress is a well-studied trigger of myriad human physiological reactions. The more familiar consequences, often considered as part of the "flight or fight" response, include increases in heart rate, blood pressure, and respirations, sweating (diaphoresis), dry mouth and throat, and bowel and bladder urgency. Less appreciated and even less understood are alterations in perception affecting the senses and thought processes. Studies conducted among members of the military and law enforcement who were involved in deadly force encounters report a multitude of perceptual distortions, although a given individual in a particular situation likely experiences just one or two of these phenomena. The most commonly described event is that of auditory exclusion or "tunnel hearing", where hearing is seemingly reduced and extremely loud sounds either are not heard or seem to be markedly diminished. In other words, certain sounds are "tuned out" under high stress. For example, a soldier involved in a gun battle with a weapon-wielding enemy combatant may not hear his gun being discharged although, in fact, he successfully fired off multiple rounds. This type of occurrence may very well explain why neither Lt. Col. Bulli nor Capt. Adler heard the impact of 0406 into the side of Elephant Mountain despite being so close by at that very instant.

Another perceptual alteration is sensory exclusion, where stress levels block one's perception of pain, even in the presence of serious personal injuries. This response may help us to understand how Jerry Adler could pick himself up after crashing to earth without benefit of a parachute, move about the ground in the vicinity of his uncontrolled landing, continue to breathe painlessly with fractured ribs, think clearly after having been rendered unconscious by forces great enough to fracture his skull, yet position himself to survive the night in subfreezing temperatures despite what would prove to be severe life-threatening injuries. It further provides insight into how Dan Bulli, despite a severely painful shattered left foot and ankle continued multiple efforts to stand and walk as he deployed his extensive survival skills.

Less commonly, individuals in high-stress life-threatening situations may experience dissociation, or the sensation that they are observers, outside of their own bodies, watching events unfold as they are experiencing them. This perceptual alteration is often accompanied by a sensation of time slowing or events transpiring in slow motion. A related phenomenon is the intrusion of bizarre thoughts into one's mind, which are often discordant with the seriousness of the situation. An example can be found in Jerry Adler's revelation as he tumbled through the air without benefit of a parachute and his subsequent thoughts while he awaited rescue. Sometimes, intrusive thoughts are not distractions, but may prove to be sources of motivation and inspiration. In the brief moment when hope wavered, both Adler and Bulli thought of their families, triggering each man to rally, refocus, and proceed to execute the tasks necessary for survival, exactly as they had been trained.

Daybreak came at 0706 on the morning of Friday January 25. Adler remained alone in the stillness. He shook off the dusting of light snow that had fallen overnight and again attempted to light a fire in the wet, snow-covered branches. As soon as he stood up and tried to take a step, he fell backward into the snow and realized he now had a new and serious problem-his left leg and foot, inside a wet pant leg and boot, were numb and hard. His booted right foot, although it remained inside the chute, had also gone cold. He couldn't untie his boots' frozen laces and their zippers were likewise stuck. Adler further lost a glove in the process of trying to get them off and again decided to stay put.

Before sunrise on Friday, January 25, a mess truck arrived from Dow and produced a most welcome hot breakfast of hot coffee, eggs, and sausage to fuel the rescue teams in preparation for the long frigid day ahead. Airborne search and rescue efforts also took off again with an SC-54, a military transport designed on the DC-4 passenger plane, departing Goose Bay, Labrador in central Newfoundland, Canada, ferrying a team of pararescuers-paramedics trained and equipped to parachute in to the crash site and provide medical care to the injured. Two helicopters departed Dow, one each originating from Otis Air Force Base on Cape Cod, Massachusetts, and Pease Air Force Base in Portsmouth, New Hampshire. In addition, a Dow-based T-33 jet trainer was inbound, along with several Bangor- and Ellsworth-based Civil Air Patrol planes.

Game Warden Pilot Stinson also returned to the air Friday morning. As he cruised over Horseshoe Pond, located at the southeastern base of Elephant Mountain, he spotted the first orange parachute. Minutes later, Warden Pilots Malcolm Maheu and George Later spotted a second chute and a man on the ground waving. Moments later at 0930, they came upon the wreckage of 0406 on the western slope of the mountain at an altitude of 1600 hundred feet, a quarter mile below the summit. Nearby, civilian pilot Bud Holt, of Holt's Flying Service located in Greenville, flew over the crash site at an altitude of 500 feet, reporting that the plane appeared to have completely disintegrated and was a quarter mile from a snow-covered trail to Horseshoe Pond. The location was 14 miles from where Robert Emery had observed the cloud of black smoke.

A flurry of activity followed the news. By mid morning, the command post in the Brownville Junction railroad offices was packed up, equipment and personnel loaded onto a convoy of vehicles, and moved 25 miles along the Katahdin Iron Works Road to the much closer and larger town of Greenville, Maine. Bill Muzzy opened his Indian Hill Motel, which had closed for the winter, to serve as the new "barracks." The new command post was established in the Inland Fisheries and Game Department office. The town's entire inventory of winter boots and tire chains were purchased to equip men and vehicles for the weather conditions.

Scott Paper Company Superintendent Fred Bigney supervised efforts to open a path to the crash site. Three company plows, operated by Malcolm Collins, Clarence "Bud" Lowe, and Harold Graham, began clearing the snow-clogged road leading to Elephant Mountain. Additional support in the form of bulldozers and bucket loaders was provided by a local construction firm, Sergeant's of Old Town. The operators broke through ten miles of forest and snow drifts up to 15 feet deep by noon to deliver rescuers from the Air Force, Air National Guard, Warden Service, Maine State Police, and local civilians to within one and one half miles of the crash site. From there, search parties trudged upward into the wilderness on snowshoes and the Sno-Travelers, though the machines had difficulty traversing the deep snow.

Bob Hume took the lead in the widest and heaviest of the three machines, breaking trail for Earlan and Wayne, who followed in the two smaller and lighter sno-travellers. The trio would spend three days in the area, opening access into the wilderness and assisting the search and rescue teams.

Two of the three Sno-Travelers brought from Millinocket, Maine to aid in the search and rescue. Manning the larger machine on the left are Dick Rideout (sitting, lt.), Bob Hume (sitting, rt.) and Earlan Campbell (standing, rear). The smaller Sno-Traveler on the right holds two unnamed searchers. (Photo courtesy of Steve Campbell)

The remains of Lt. Col. Joe R. Simpson and Maj. William Gabriel were the first to be found. Helicopters were unable to assist in their recovery because of the high winds. Moreover, down drafts created by their rotors created even more blowing snow, further impeding ground personnel. Unable to carry the two lost fliers through the drifting snow, the searchers retraced their steps, slogging back through the snow to the trailhead, and by nightfall had returned safely to the command post.

The smaller of the two Sno-Travelers previously pictured was fully restored by Steve Campbell, one of Earlan's three sons. The completely operable machine is on display as part of the collection of antique snowmobiles in the Millinocket snowmobiling museum, co-founded by Steve. (Photo by author)

Early in the morning of January 25, TSgt. Eugene "Slab" Slabinski was on duty in western Cape Cod, Massachusetts at the 551st Air Force Hospital, Otis Air Force Base. Slabinski had previously served in the Army's famed 82nd Airborne Division as a parachutist until 1952, later joining the Air Force in 1954. He was ultimately assigned as a parachutist-rescuer to a rescue squadron. When his squadron was later dissolved, Slab was assigned as a hospital paramedic, though he remained ready to deploy at a moments notice on pararescue missions. Notice came when he was ordered to urgently grab his gear and head to the helicopter flight line. He was on his way to northern Maine.

He boarded the assigned Sikorsky CH3-B chopper, serial number 62-1257, joining the crew of aircraft commander, Captain Kenneth L. Winden, Co-pilot First Lieutenant Edward L. Heft and crew chiefs Staff Sergeant (SSgt.) John Pappas, and Airman Anthony Scolaro. They took off at 0430 and headed directly to Dow Air Force Base in Bangor, Maine, arriving at 0630. The aircraft was refueled while the pilots received a briefing on the search area and the others loaded winter survival gear for each crewmember. Lifting off again at 0730, they headed to their assigned area, finding no signs of the wreck of 0406 after an hour of searching. A radio transmission from the on-scene search controller then reported that a parachute had been spotted on the ground by a civilian aircraft.

Heft called in their position and requested directions to the chute, approximately 12 nautical miles away. Winden and Heft wound their way through the valleys, avoiding turbulence and a series of snow showers that obscured the ridgelines. Their navigation equipment was useless at the low altitude and the map guiding them did not show the contour of the land below. Nonetheless, on they flew. When the helo arrived within three miles of the sighting, they passed over the scene controller who vectored them in to the chute's location, where they hovered.

The pilots assessed that the winds were at 20 to 25 knots with moderate turbulence. Visibility was one to two miles through hazy skies. Slabinski slipped into his "horse collar,," a sling placed over his head and under his arms, which was then hitched to the chopper's cable hoist. Clutching his gear, he was lowered to the ground as close to the chute as the pilots dared. As the crew watched, Slab signaled to be raised back up – the snow was above his waist, making it impossible for him to move to the flyer, who was suspended by his parachute ten feet up a tree. However, like Winden and Heft above, he could see that Bob Morrison, still harnessed in his chute, had not survived the landing.

As they continued the search, the crew eyed a second chute further down the slope. Winden circled the spot. Below, Dan Bulli heard the chopper's approach. He could make out the Sikorsky's bulbous bright red nose and trim tapered tail, although it's dark green fuselage was obscured by the towering, verdant fir trees. As the aircraft appeared overhead, Bulli waved one arm and signaled with his mirror. The chopper hovered between 40 and 50 yards away, lowering Slabinski for the second time. He trudged ahead, grasping overhanging branches and pulling himself up and through the snow, finally reaching Bulli. He opened a can of water for the downed pilot to drink and administered a morphine injection to treat Bulli's pain. He radioed his crew, letting them know that the situation on the ground was under control.

Winden and Heft, knowing that Slabinski would need some time to ready the flier for evacuation, whirled in larger and larger circles searching for additional chutes. After flying in the area for 15 minutes and not finding any, they passed over the ridge and surveyed the charred landscape, finding a partially burned chute among the debris, but no nearby flyer. Catching sight of a light civilian plane, they pursued it to a fourth chute. Circling once, the crew spotted its intended passenger enveloped in its folds. Jerry Adler saw the helo pass overhead. As it circled a second time, the rescuers could see him weakly move his head and wave one hand.

After splinting Bulli's left leg, Slab loaded him onto the remnants of the life raft and dragged him to where the trees were thinnest. Having found Adler, the chopper radioed Slabinski, who confirmed that he was ready with Bulli for the pickup. Winden and Heft flew back to Slabinski's location where a crew chief threaded the rescue basket through a break in the trees barely large enough to accommodate the apparatus. Slabinski helped Bulli aboard and signaled the crew to raise the pilot. As the basket containing the flier was hoisted, it began to spin wildly in the downwash from the aircraft's spinning blades. Winden and Heft struggled against the turbulence to keep the chopper hovering in place as Bulli was raised toward the side door. The two crew chiefs grabbed the basket and drew him inside. Next, the horse collar was lowered and Slabinski was hoisted back up to rejoin his crewmates.

Slab's assessment told him that Bulli's condition was stable enough to tolerate the hop back over the ridge to pick up Adler, who according to the pilots, appeared to be in extremis. The chopper flew back over the ridge, this time hovering over Adler. Again, the pilots fought the turbulence to remain in position. On went the collar and down went Slabinski. The rescue basket followed, snapping branches along the way as it was maneuvered through the trees. As anticipated, Adler was in poor shape from shock and exposure. As Slab would later describe, Adler's frostbitten ankles and feet were "like a marble statue." Slabinski loaded him into the basket and signaled the chopper crew to hoist away. Once Adler was safely on board, the cable was lowered for Slab, who once again was brought back up in the horse collar. The pilots revved the engine, lowered the nose, and banked to the southeast, racing toward Bangor and Dow Air Force Base, 50 miles away.

As soon as the helo touched down at 1105, an airman waved Winden across the snow-fringed tarmac to the front of a low-slung two-story brick building capped by a lettered sign identifying it as the home of "Base Operations". Standing by and observing operations were Brigadier General Alvan C. Gillen II, Commander, 57th Air Division, SAC and Major General James H. Walsh, Deputy Commander, 8th Air Force, SAC, who had travelled from Westover. A drab green field ambulance idled close by, its solitary red dome light slowly revolving above the driver's compartment, a beacon piercing the brilliant winter sunshine. Two medics hustled a canvas pole stretcher to the chopper's open side door where they were greeted by Gene Slabinski, wearing a pile-lined leather hat and a broad smile topped by an equally broad red moustache. Slab stepped aside, allowing the medics to collect Jerry Adler and transfer him to the waiting ambulance. Four others jogged over with a second stretcher for Bulli who was placed alongside his crewmate for the short ride to the small 50-bed base hospital. Meanwhile, as the chopper was refueled, Slabinski headed into the hospital to replenish his supplies and medications. He and his crew had one final mission to fly that day– the recovery of Bob Morrison.

Once the Sikorsky was refueled and Slabinski was provisioned, the Otis-based crew departed from Dow, delivering Slabinski over Morrison's location. Slab was lowered to the ground by collar and cable, this time with both snowshoes and a radio that had been provided during the latest Dow layover. These two items were about to become extremely valuable assets for the pararescuer, for when he radioed the chopper to lower the rescue basket, he was informed that the hoist cable had broken. The basket was not coming down. Of greater concern, Slabinski was not going back up.

The CH3B headed back to Dow, leaving Slab in the snow to fend for himself until either another chopper could rescue the rescuer or until such time as ground-based rescuers could make their way to his location. He snowshoed to the tree from which Morrison remained suspended by his parachute. Next, Slabinski managed to climb the tree high enough to reach Morrison's seat and release its survival kit and sleeping bag. He then set up under the pines, lighting a fire, which quickly warmed him, and settled into the sleeping bag for the night, keeping watch over the Major's remains. Ground rescuers arrived on site the next morning, January 26, and assisted

Slabinski in recovering Bob Morrison's body. An H43 helicopter from Dow manned by the Maine Air National Guard then arrived overhead, lifting first Morrison and then Slab on board before returning to Dow.

At sunrise on Saturday, January 26, the contingent involved in the search, rescue, and recovery of 0406 and its crew continued its work. Ground searchers, including seven members of the Maine Air National Guard-Team leader Master Sergeant (MSgt.) Leo Gilmore, Assistant leader Staff Sergeant James Bennett, MSgts. Paul Tower and Richard Gaudet, TSgt. Roland Andrews, and SSgts. Elmer Kitchen and Joel Shorette, followed the path back to the grim crash scene. There they recovered the remains of Maj. Hill, Capt. Hanson, and Capt. Leuchter, along with those of Simpson and Gabriel after their discovery near the remnants of the fuselage's crew compartment. Those of TSgt. O'Keefe were found within the aft section of the plane, still secured in the tail gunner's compartment. The six downed warriors' remains were gently lifted onto sleds for the slow difficult journey down off the mountain. Only the rescuer's labored breathing and the *squeak crunch* of the heavily laden sleds straining against the snow punctuated the sound of the wind. By midday, the group completed its descent and reached the road where ambulances awaited to transport the crew's remains. The lost airmen arrived at Dow via ambulance and helicopter later that afternoon.

7

At Home

The Bullis

Despite the frequent moves associated with military life, Westover, like many military bases, responded to the lifestyle's challenges by forming a tightly knit community. Notifications of the flyers' families happened quickly during the late afternoon of January 24. Ev Bulli was at home with her two recuperating children. The doorbell rang just before 1700 as she was leaning over the kitchen sink washing dishes. She stopped scrubbing, dried her hands, and opened the front door, surprised, but pleased to see Lt. Col. Enoch Broyles and his wife Jane, close family friends. She greeted them warmly, inviting them out of the bitter cold, taking their coats, and showing them to the living room. The thought briefly struck her that it was unusual for them to be visiting at such an odd hour, but she was happy for a respite from her chores. After the usual greetings and small talk, a silence settled over the trio. Enoch spoke first, "Evelyn, we have to tell you that Dan is missing."

Confused, after short pause Ev replied "No he's not. He's flying today." That only bought her a tiny bit more time to process what she had really just heard. Broyles went on to explain that Bulli's plane had likely crashed. He provided the few details that were known so far- that 0406 not been in radio contact for some time, that a logger had witnessed the last few moments of the flight, and saw the telltale column of smoke once the plane went out of sight. She braced herself for the worst possible news while clinging to a thread of hope for her husband's survival. Ev maintained her composure for the sake of her children who had come from their rooms to see their unannounced visitors. She gently explained the situation to eleven year-old John and nine year-old Marilyn, both of whom had overheard parts of the adults' conversation.

Evelyn, numbed by the gut-wrenching news, felt like an outsider watching events unfold from afar. The following hours brought a blurred whirlwind of activity to the Bulli home. A parade of uniformed and non-uniformed personnel and friends filtered through. The base chaplain gently consoled her, "There is so little I can do, so little I can say." The family minister, wing commander and his wife, squadron commander and his wife, and neighbors and friends by the dozen visited, offering expressions of caring support and concern in hushed tones. To an outsider, the scene took on the atmosphere of a funeral, though it was not at all clear whether or not one would soon follow for the family.

John was sent off to his room at an hour much later than his usual bedtime. Before nodding off to sleep, he looked at the plastic Revell model B-52 that he had built, which was now suspended from the ceiling over his bed and thought, "What could have happened to Dad's plane?" Ev's night was far from over. "Around midnight, after everyone had left, I went out into the driveway and stood, alone. I remember feeling vaguely surprised, and somewhat bitter that, despite the events of the past eight hours, things looked exactly as they had the night before. The stars were brilliant in an endless black sky, and over across the river valley, lights twinkled softly on Mt. Holyoke. The sky was piercingly intense, and I turned and went back into the warm house we loved."

The longest night of Evelyn Bulli's life passed at a staggeringly slow pace, the seconds ticking off the mantle clock passed like minutes. The following morning, television and radio news reports offered continuous updates on the search and rescue, most of them devastatingly erroneous and conflicting. Ev listened to one such broadcast at 0700 announcing the discovery of the wreckage with no survivors found. Thoughtfully, a local school tutor, Mrs. Brown, offered to tend to John for the morning.

Off they went, escaping the snow and cold as they stepped in to the otherworldly warmth, humidity, and greenery contained within the Mount Holyoke College greenhouse. The exotic surroundings and plant species quickly engaged the inquisitive eleven year-old's mind. The worries and uncertainties of home, which until now had always been a source of predictable comfort and stability, were left at the door.

Fortunately, the Broyles had returned to remain with Ev, while Enoch received regular updates on the status of the search on the Bulli residence's telephone. Approaching 1000, the phone rang yet again. Broyles took the call informing all that the crash site had been found. Impossibly, the tension ratcheted unbearably upward. Soon after, he answered the next call and gently informed Ev that a survivor had been sighted. She "couldn't dare hope that out of nine men, that one would be my husband." More news came just before noon as John returned home from his adventure. Enoch lifted the receiver to his ear before the end of the first ring. Ev could not see his face from the next room, but as he continued to listen, he extended his arm around the corner, touching the tips of his thumb and forefinger together while extending the remaining fingers to form the "ok" sign.

With conflicting emotions, she sensitively observed, "For us, the waiting was over. For the families of seven others, it would never end." Neighbors quickly arrived at the Bulli home. John and Marilyn were each whisked off to stay with friends. Ev scrambled to pack some clothes and personal belongings and immediately headed to Bangor, Dow Air Force Base Hospital, and her husband. There she would remain until his release and eventual return to Westover.

The Hansons

Wanda Hanson was home awaiting Herb's return on the evening of January 24. She was used to his irregular schedule and late returning flights, so was not too surprised that he had not yet stepped through the door by supper hour. She heard a knock on the front door and opened it to find

Frank Wirth. He and his wife, Gert, were neighbors and close friends of the Hansons. Wirth broke the news that Herb's plane was missing.

Upstairs in her room, fifteen year-old Trish overheard the two adults speaking in hushed tones and listened, hearing that her father's "plane went down". Wanda gathered herself and explained as best she could to their youngest daughter. Sam remembers, "I knew immediately that he would not be back. Six year-olds don't really have much grasp on death, but I knew. So I went and laid on his side of their bed, and listened to people come and go. And Skeeter Davis must have been in the top ten with 'The End of the World'. It kept playing on the radio!" Wirth took Sam to his home to be with Gert and their daughter, Mary Bridget, while Wanda waited and managed the arrivals and departures of well-wishers. Seventeen year-old Deana was picked up from a student council meeting at school and joined the others at home, where she learned of the missing flight.

Wanda called her parents, Fred and Moraha Dean living in Rapid City, South Dakota, to notify them of the afternoon's news. Fred immediately made arrangements to fly east to be with his daughter and granddaughters. He arrived early in the afternoon of Friday, January 25. Just as her father walked through the door of the house, Wanda received the news of Herb's death. It was her thirty-eighth birthday.

As word of the crash and fate of the crew spread, the local media began to gather outside, photographing the Hanson home. Following a brief discussion with Wanda, Frank Wirth quickly took the girls away from the growing chaos to stay with friends. Three days later, Fred Dean was on the road with Wanda, Deana, Trish, and Sam, heading home to South Dakota.

Frank Wirth followed by train, serving as the honor guard accompanying Herb's remains on the trip home to Rapid City.

Trish described the shock and trauma of these days and those that followed, "I also remember someone taking me to school to get my things...I spoke with Mrs. Pasternak (her teacher) outside in the hall...but I was not able to go into the classroom...too traumatized I think. So, I never really said goodbye to my friends...we were outta there in what 3 days or so with Grandpa Dean driving us across country. I remember nothing about that trip. Then, when we got to Rapid (City) and had to go through the funeral...I just could not keep it together...I think I fainted at the funeral home, then we went out to the national cemetery, the flyover, the whole thing...completely overwhelming. Then we went back to the (Pretty Pines) Party House (Fred and Moraha Dean's catering hall business) for people to gather and eat...and I remember looking and thinking...I can't believe these people are talking and laughing as if nothing happened...my dad is dead!"

The Hills

At the Hill home, Mildred, too, was expecting her husband Bob to arrive shortly. As if on cue, the family beagle, Tippy, took up his usual position by the front door to welcome him home. When Tippy soon began barking, Roberta, their 14 year-old daughter, glanced outside to see a vehicle parked at the curb and two Air Force officers heading up the sidewalk. After being notified that Bob's plane was missing, the waiting began. It continued until the following day, when the family was told of his death and arrangements were made to return to Joplin, Missouri. Bob Frank, a close friend and co-pilot from Hill's previous crew, escorted Bob's casket home to Joplin.

Bob Hill and crew at Westover AFB, 1960-1961. Hill is kneeling (front row, left). Immediately behind him and standing is close friend and co-pilot, Bob Frank. (Photo courtesy of Roberta Hill)

Meanwhile, Tippy kept his nightly vigil, remaining unrewarded, as his home slowly emptied of guests, friends, and eventually belongings. His watch ended when he left with Mildred and Bobbie three days later, and what had been his home once again became a house, devoid of any trace of the Hills having ever lived there.

Bob Hill and daughter Bobbie's dog Tippy. Tippy would wait each evening by the front door for Bob's return home, undated. (Photo courtesy of Roberta Hill)

The O'Keefe's

Freshly grieving the loss of her husband, Anna O'Keefe, mother of TSgt. Michael O'Keefe, was spending the night of January 24, 1963 at the Brooklyn home of her son, John. That evening's television news reported the downing of a B-52 over Maine. A wave of apprehension fell over her as she thought of her son, Michael, and soon she after went to sleep. Being away from her home would not delay Anna from receiving the news that indeed Michael was on board the lost flight, for unlike the families at Westover, there would be no staff car pulling up to her home bearing military officers in uniform, no knock on her door after which they would break the news, and no accompanying chaplain to support her when she collapsed.

Anna May (Joyce) O'Keefe, Michael's mother, undated. (Photo courtesy of Theresa Bailey)

Richard O'Keefe, Anna's oldest son, was startled awake by the sound of the building's door buzzer reverberating in his Bronx apartment on the Grand Concourse. Next to him, his wife, Anita, stirred while his two children remained soundly asleep. He glanced at the bedside clock, which informed him that the time was 0200 and wondered who could possibly be ringing at that hour. Richard groggily threw on a robe and slippers, and headed downstairs to the building's entrance. A Western Union courier waited with a telegram addressed to him. He signed for the delivery and headed back upstairs, wondering what message worthy of a telegram would roust him at that hour. Once inside the apartment, he carefully unfolded the small yellow piece of paper.

"IT IS WITH DEEP REGRET THAT I OFFICIALLY INFORM YOU THAT YOU BROTHER, TSGT MICHAEL F. O'KEEFE, IS MISSING ON A ROUTINE FLIGHT FROM WESTOVER AFB, MASS., SINCE APPROXIMATELY 5:30 P.M. 24 JAN 63. REQUEST YOU NOTIFY YOUR MOTHER SINCE I UNDERSTAND SHE IS IN ILL HEALTH DUE TO RECENT DEATH OF YOUR FATHER. DUE TO THIS I FELT THAT DIRECT NOTIFICATION TO HER WOULD NOT BE ADVISABLE. AN EXTENSIVE SEARCH IS NOW BEING CONDUCTED. WHEN FURTHER INFORMATION IS RECEIVED, YOU WILL BE NOTIFIED IMMEDIATELY. A LETTER CONTAINING FURTHER DETAILS WILL BE FORWARDED TO YOU AT THE EARLIEST POSSIBLE DATE. PLEASE ACCEPT MY SINCERE SYMPATHY AT THIS TIME OF ANXIETY. COMMANDER

WESTOVER AFB, MASS. COMMANDER 57 AIR DIV WESTOVER
AFB, MASS.

O'Keefe's stomach sank as he sat at his kitchen table, gently holding the
telegram and staring at the declaration of uncertainty regarding his youngest
sibling that he would now have to share with his close knit family in their
sorrow. Richard hesitantly reached for the phone, knowing that the O'Keefe
family was facing a tortured sleepless night ahead. "It was," he declared, "the
worst night of my life." The ringing woke John, who picked up and received
the news from Rich. Anna, too, awoke, and immediately associated the
interruption with her earlier premonition precipitated by the television news
regarding Michael. The O'Keefes gathered at Richard and Anita's home,
focusing on one television, four radios tuned to different stations, and the
telephone, which sat silently on a small table, desperate for an update on
Mike's status. The family heard and saw the same maddeningly conflicting
news reports as Evelyn Bulli. John and Rich called Westover repeatedly,
receiving no information other than instructions to await word.

Friday evening, word was received that two survivors and two casualties
had been found, but Mike was not among them. As five crewmen were still
missing, hopes were buoyed that "if he had gotten out he would be found in
the next few hours and rushed to a hospital and everything would be alright."
News broadcasts offered no additional information. There was no further
contact from Westover on Friday night or Saturday. The O'Keefe's were
physically and emotionally spent. Their situation became unimaginably worse
when at 1920 on Saturday, the door buzzer in Richard's apartment once

again summoned him downstairs where another Western Union courier awaited. The burly warehouse worker hesitated, then signed for the telegram. He turned and stepped back inside, slowly climbed the stairs, and entered his apartment. He considered the yellow telegram for a moment, then opened and unfolded the message, all hope for his youngest brother now dashed.

"IT IS WITH DEEP REGRET THAT I INFORM YOU OF THE =DEATH OF YOUR BROTHER, TSGT MICHAEL F. O'KEEFE WHO WAS PREVIOUSLY=REPORTED MISSING. HE DIED AS A RESULT OF A MILITARY AIRCRAFT =ACCIDENT ON 24 JAN 63. A LETTER CONTAINING FURTHER DETAILS =WILL BE SENT TO YOU AT THE EARLIEST POSSIBLE DATE. PLEASE ACCEPT =MY SINCERE SYMPATHY IN YOUR BEREAVEMENT. SIGNED COMMANDER =WESTOVER AIR FORCE BASE MASSACHUSETTS"

Richard again bore the lonely and dreaded responsibility of informing his family with even more terrible news, washing away their hopes and replacing them with renewed and unimaginable grief. His mother, Anna, was inconsolable. His sister Agnes, seven months pregnant, was hysterical. Anita described her emotions as "running around in circles." According to her, Rich too, was understandably "in very bad shape." The family now entered a yet another lengthy wait, pending word regarding the return of Mike's remains. And still, no one from the Air Force called or came to the door.

The phone finally rang on Tuesday, January 29 around 2000 that Mike's casket was to be shipped home by train to New York in the next two hours, accompanied by his friend and barracks-mate of seven years as the honor guard. Rich and John met the train bearing their younger brother's remains at New York's Pennsylvania Station at 0325 on the morning of January 30, staying together with Mike until they reached the John P. Dunn funeral home. There, Rich and John agreed to open the casket to be sure that it did, in fact, contain Mike's remains. After confirming Michael's identity, Rich carefully removed Mike's wings from his uniform to preserve as a memento. The brothers agreed that the funeral visitation would be closed-casket.

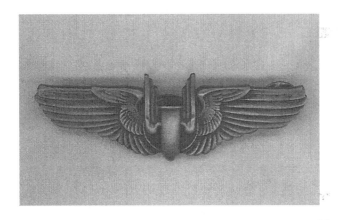

Mike O'Keefe's uniform wings retrieved by his brother Richard on January 30, 1963. (Photo courtesy of Theresa Bailey)

On Monday, February 4, for the second time in 11 days, Anna O'Keefe, her family, and friends made the hour and one-half long journey to the Long Island National Cemetery in Farmingdale, New York. For the second time in 11 days, the same gravesite yawned open to receive an O'Keefe. For the second time in 11 days they endured a military funeral officiated by the same honor guard, the first for the eldest and the second for the youngest O'Keefe to serve his nation. For the second time in 11 days, a sobbing Anna wearing the same black mourning dress, listened to the haunting notes of "Taps" and was formally yet gently handed another folded American flag that had draped a loved one's casket. As the service came to a close, a jet streaked overhead, a fitting tribute to Michael, the family would later agree.

The Morrisons

Seventeen year-old high school senior Shari Morrison was working in a West Springfield china store on January 24 when an Air Force officer pulled up in a staff car, with her brother Max already in the vehicle. The officer informed her that she was need at home as "there had been crash and were looking for the plane my father had been flying. I was in shock! When I arrived home my mother was in tears and …they didn't know if anyone had survived. It was awful not knowing until the next day when the wreckage was found that there were only two survivors, and my dad was not one of them." Irene, Max recounted, "took it so hard that they put her on tranquilizers for a while." He, too, was deeply affected at just 16 years of age, "I dreamt every night about my dad – that's how close I was. And I kept dreaming that he was going to come out of the woods and be a hero. Of course that never happened." Irene opted not to have the children attend Bob's funeral in Dodge City, Kansas, though they would later attend the memorial service at Westover. The impact on Max was striking, as he recalled, "I didn't get closure because my mother didn't take us to the funeral."

The Adlers and The Leuchters

Capt. Richard Neveu was the electronic warfare officer assigned to standardization crew S-47, along with Morrison, Snyder, Adler, and Leuchter. It was in his usual seat that Jerry Adler had been sitting aboard 0406. On the afternoon of January 24, Neveu received a call to report to the wing commander in his dress blue uniform. Knowing that something unusual was up, but not what, he presented as ordered. Neveu was informed that 0406 was missing and that he was to proceed to Jerry Adler's home and officially notify his wife, Sonnie. He headed to the Adlers' home, accompanied by a female personal affairs officer. After parking their vehicle, the two headed up the walk to the front door.

Sonnie was in the kitchen preparing dinner for seven year-old Sheree and four year-old Karen when the doorbell rang. She stopped working and headed through the living room to greet the caller. Sheree and Karen were right behind her. When Sonnie opened the door to find Richard in his dress uniform, accompanied by a female officer that she did not recognize, she screamed and began sobbing before either officer uttered a word. Karen knew that "It must be something about Daddy." Neveu caught Sonnie as her knees buckled but before she could hit the floor, and helped her to the living room sofa, attempting to console her as best as he could.

His compatriot gathered the girls and headed back to the kitchen, intending to complete preparing the meal that Sonnie had begun just moments earlier. The girls, though, huddled together next to the doorway, trying to glean tidbits from the living room conversation. Sheree recalled that all that could be understood from the adults' conversation was Neveu explaining to their mother "…the plane had gone off the radar…" Sonnie quickly gathered herself and began the arduous wait for word on her husband's fate. Ken Snyder later arrived to spend time with Sonnie, relieving Neveu and the personal affairs officer. Later that evening, Ken headed over to the Leuchter residence to support Charlie's wife, Georgia, and their children. On the 25th, the Adler family received word of Jerry's rescue. The Leuchter family was informed of Charlie's death.

Heartbreaking scenes unfolded across the country as the notifications were completed and funerals were organized. In the days before and after the funerals, each of the surviving widows and Anna O'Keefe would receive personal letters of sympathy and appreciation from Dan Bulli, Col. Edward Nichols, Commander of the 99th Bombardment Wing at Westover, Brigadier General Alvan Gillam II, Commander of the 57th Air Division at Westover, General Thomas Power, Commander of SAC, General Curtis LeMay, Air Force Chief of Staff, and President John F. Kennedy, Commander in Chief. Only much later would the missives provide their recipients any solace.

8

Recuperation and Healing

Following admission to the 860th Medical Group Hospital at Dow, both Bulli and Adler remained sedated. Dan Bulli's injuries included the lacerations he received during his ejection and parachute landing, multiple fractures of his left foot and ankle, and a spinal compression fracture from his helmet smashing into the escape hatch during ejection. He would require a total of four surgeries over the ensuing five months to repair his foot and ankle fractures. The remaining injuries would eventually mend themselves, though they would serve as constant nagging reminders for the rest of his life.

Jerry Adler remained unconscious, even after the sedation wore off. In addition to the injuries incurred by his remarkable landing, he was now additionally suffering from pneumonia in both lungs, likely the result of cold-induced lung injury compounded by impaired breathing caused by the multiple rib fractures. Adler was further battling the frostbite afflicting his toes, feet, and left leg. After three days in the hospital, in became clear that his condition required a higher level of care than could be provided at Dow. He was transferred to the local major civilian hospital, Eastern Maine General Hospital, the state's second largest hospital. Adler would not regain consciousness until five days after the crash.

Both flyers continued to recuperate, albeit slowly. By February 6, though still requiring ongoing hospitalization, they were sufficiently stable to receive orders to be flown back to Massachusetts. The two crewmates were reunited on February 11 as they were placed on board a medical evacuation flight from Dow to Westover. The hospital to which they were headed was a relatively new state-of-the-art facility built in 1956 at a cost of $3.5 million with a staff of more than 400 health care personnel. Ev Bulli poignantly described the scene as Dan Bulli and Jerry Adler returned home.

"I walked at the side of the stretcher as he was carried from the plane down a canvas-covered ramp and from the crowd gathered, hushed people, out two children came forward toward the waiting ambulance. Someone had thoughtfully gone to the homes in South Hadley, Massachusetts where I had hurriedly left them, and brought them to the base to greet their father. When they reached out and touched his hand, it brought tears to the eyes of two people who thought they had long since exhausted all emotion.

"It was raining that night, unusual indeed for Massachusetts in February, and although there was still much snow on the ground, somehow there seemed a hint of spring in the air. I think what I remember most about that night was quiet. So many had come out just to stand in hushed respectful silence. The ambulance, with its red light clicking softly in the rain, waited until my husband and Capt. Adler were put inside, and then it made its way slowly toward the Westover hospital. And so began the end of the most trying twenty-one days in our lives."

Dan Bulli had several duties to fulfill despite his injuries and slow recovery. His first order of business was to give thanks to those directly responsible for his rescue. Strengthened by his improving health, on February 24th Bulli requested a typewriter and paper. The clattering of the keys could be heard outside his room in the 814th Medical Group (SAC) hospital as he began to type:

"Commander

551 Air Base Squadron

Helicopter Detachment

Otis AFB, Mass

Dear Sir,

"I would like to formally express my gratitude to your crew that rescued me and one of my crew members from the Maine woods last month, subsequent to the crash of my B-52. The crew was composed of Capt. Kenneth Winden, Lt. Edward Heft, Sgt. Eugene Slabinski, and two other airmen whose names I was unable to obtain.

"Your boys certainly earn their money. They had that whirly bird sitting right in the treetops while I was being hoisted up in the basket. When I saw Sgt. Slabinski and his handle bar mustache come plowing through that chest deep snow I knew everything was under control and began to relax.

"As a token of my appreciation I would like to send each of five men an engraved cigarette lighter. Would you be kind enough to confirm their names so that I may do this when released from the hospital?

"Both Capt. Adler and myself are progressive satisfactorily. I should be back on my feet by May, but Capt. Adler's frostbitten feet may keep him down a bit longer.

"Although I have personally expressed my thanks to your crew, I would feel remiss if I did not take this opportunity to advise you of the kindness and consideration that your men demonstrated to me.

"Sincerely,

(signed) D. E. Bulli

Lt. Col., USAF"

The following day, he began crafting a series of letters, each of which required much deeper thought to compose and provoked far more pain than his constellation of physical injuries. He sat up at the typewriter and scrolled in a fresh sheet of paper.

"Dear Wanda,

"I've been wanting to write to you for quite some time, but it was only the other day that Evelyn got your address from Charlotte.

"We are glad to hear that you are getting settled in Rapid City and that you have moved into your new house.

"Things here are slowly getting back to normal. The doctors tell me that if things go right I may be back on my feet by May. I went a full day without medication yesterday and am beginning to feel half normal again.

"There isn't much I can say about the accident, Wanda. Things happened so quickly and at so low an altitude that Herb had no time for fear or pain.

"I wanted you to know that the accident board found that there was nothing humanly possible which could have been done by any of us in the airplane to prevent the accident. Just seconds before it occurred, Herb called me on the interphone and told me that it would soon be time to turn back eastward. I am sure that when the accident happened he was refining his estimated turn time.

"It is difficult to express how I feel about the whole thing. While we were together socially only infrequently, Herb occupied a special place in my heart. He was my ideal of what a man should be. I admired and respected him so much, that to a small degree, I think I know how much his being gone means to you and the girls.

"Ev and I think of you constantly. We hope that time and faith in the Lord will help you fill the void which has been left by Herb's absence.

"Sincerely,

(signed) Dan"

The letter to Wanda Hanson was followed by similar letters of condolence and support to Anna O'Keefe and each of Bulli's lost crewmen's surviving spouses. These tasks completed, the very next day, February 26, he helped celebrate his son John's twelfth birthday from his hospital bed. No one could possibly imagine the emotions that whipsawed behind the steady, controlled countenance of Dan Bulli. He was released from the hospital on March 1, thirty-four days following his rescue.

On February 26, 1963 Lt. Col. Dan Bulli helped celebrate son, John's twelfth birthday from his Westover hospital bed with daughter Marilyn (lt.) and John (rt.). (Photo courtesy of John Bulli)

Bulli received a response to his letter, dated 5 March 1963, from the Officer in Charge (OIC) of Helicopter Operations at Otis Air Force Base:

"Dear Colonel Bulli

"Your letter of 24 February concerning personnel assigned to the Helicopter Flight was received with pleasure.

"We have discussed on several occasions how you and Capt. Adler were getting along. It is good to hear that both of you are on the road to recovery, and we send our best wishes.

"The CH-3B Helicopter, one used to pick you up, is one of six helicopters assigned to Otis for Texas Tower support. We feel that it is the finest helicopter in production today, and enables us to provide faster service under more adverse conditions. We are always ready to assist in any distress.

" The crew that participated in your crash rescue has been submitted for the Sikorsky Flying Safety Award. The award is presented to the individual by the Sikorsky Aircraft Company, Hartford, Connecticut.

"The rescue crew was composed of the following personnel:

Captain Kenneth L. Winden- pilot

1ˢᵗ Lieutenant Edward L. Heft-co-pilot

TSgt Eugene S. Slabinski-Paramedic

SSgt John G. Pappas-Crew Chief

A1c Anthony Scolaro-Assistant crew chief

"We would like to invite you and Captain Adler to visit Otis Air Force Base and have another helicopter ride. This time, we will take you out to see one of the Texas Towers before they are dismantled.

" The boys will certainly appreciate your cigarette lighters and carry them with pride.

"Sincerely,

(signed) Edward A. Hook

Major, USAF

OIC, Helicopter Operations"

The "Texas Towers" to which Maj. Hook referred were a series of off-shore platforms housing radar domes that served as part of early the nation's early warning systems for incoming air attacks on the eastern United States. Based on oil platforms in the Gulf of Mexico, and hence their name, five such platforms were originally planned, although only three, numbers 2, 3, and 4, were ever actually constructed. The towers, located off the coasts of New Jersey, Cape Cod, and Nantucket, were full operational from 1958-1963. One of the three structures, Tower 4, sunk during a storm on January 15, 1961, resulting in the death of the 28 servicemen and civilian contractors manning the station. The remaining two stations were decommissioned and dismantled in 1963.

True to his word, Dan Bulli ensured that each crewmember of the rescue helicopter received an engraved lighter that was personalized with his rank, name, and the inscription

"THANKS FOR THE LIFT

25 JAN 63

LT COL BULLI"

And true to his word, Major Hook saw that each crewmember received the Helicopter Rescue Award from Sikorsky Aircraft. Understandably, neither Bulli nor Adler took him up on his offer of another helicopter ride.

TSgt. Eugene Slabinski, USAF (rt.) receiving the Sikorsky Helicopter Rescue award. (Photo courtesy of Dolores Moleski)

Jerry Adler remained hospitalized at Westover. While his fractures continued to mend and he recovered from the bilateral pneumonia, the combined infections and extreme cold exposure likely contributed to the chronic lung disease from which he would suffer for the rest of his life. By April, the frostbite affecting Adler's toes and left foot could no longer be safely observed while the doctors hoped for continued improvement or resolution. Surgeons at first removed several toes on each foot. Following surgery, complications arose and his left foot developed an infection. The poor circulation resulting from the frostbite prevented antibiotics from travelling to and penetrating the infected tissues. Gangrene set in and Adler's left leg had to be amputated below the knee. Ultimately, the remaining toes of his right foot also had to be removed.

The infection and frostbite treated, on July 1, 1963, Jerry was flown to Lackland Air Force Base near San Antonio, Texas to continue specialized medical care at the Wilford Hall Air Force Hospital. There he would receive a prosthesis for his left leg, a specially designed shoe to accommodate his right foot, and undergo extensive rehabilitation. After ten years, eight months and twenty-four days of honorable active military service, Capt. Gerald J. Adler, USAF was medically discharged from the Air Force on March 21, 1964.

During his lengthy hospital stay and recuperation, Jerry Adler, like Dan Bulli, entered an extended period of contemplation. Although manifestly thankful for his good fortune in having lived through the crash, he did not dwell on his own survival or even the consequences of his serious injuries. Rather, he turned his focus outward and committed himself to the welfare of the surviving spouses and children of his fallen comrades. However, the means by which to achieve these goals was at first unclear. A relative, who happened to be an attorney, suggested that one potential pathway could be found through the courts, and referred Adler to the law firm of Kreindler and Kreindler, located in Manhattan.

Harry Kreindler founded the practice in 1950. The second Kreindler in the firm was Harry's son, Lee, a graduate of Dartmouth College and Harvard Law School. The younger Kreindler specialized as a plaintiff's attorney in aviation law, and already enjoyed a reputation as a leader in the field. He was on the verge of publishing "Aviation Accident Law," a three-volume text that would soon become the definitive treatise on the subject. After reviewing the circumstances surrounding the accident, Lee Kreindler agreed to take the case. First, however, he needed plaintiffs to represent.

Adler, like Bulli, carefully crafted thoughtful letters expressing his sympathy and hopes for their futures to Doris Simpson, Doris Gabriel, Mildred Hill, Georgia Leuchter, Irene Morrison, Wanda Hanson, and Anna O'Keefe. He also shared his thoughts, the result of much consideration and many detailed conversations, as to how their futures and those of their children might be secured. On June 28, 1963 he penned his letter to Wanda Hanson on sheets of hospital letterhead.

"Dear Wanda,

"We met only once, at the standboard party last December, but I feel akin to you as I do to Mildred Hill whom I met here at the hospital and all the other wives who survived our crash whether I knew them or not. Dan has kept me informed of you and your children, of Herb's promotion, and it was he who gave me your address. Today is his day to leave for Maxwell. He is doing very well although walking with a noticeable limp.

"As you can see I am still in the hospital but will be leaving for the Lackland AFB Hospital Monday. My loss of one leg below the knee and the toes of the other foot pales into insignificance beside your loss. I only hope and pray that all is going well with you and yours now. At Lackland I will be getting a new leg, a special shoe, will finish healing and convalescing, meet a retirement board and then return to my wife's hometown of Houston. She and my daughters leave for there Sunday.

"Wanda, this letter although long overdue, has been awaiting answers to many questions. These answers are now in. And so with the knowledge and approval of many people including Dan Bulli and Irene Morrison, I take pen in hand now in a letter very similar to one I have just finished to Mildred. With this idea just getting off the ground we already have two commitments and I think we'll have seven, shortly, to participate in a negligence suit against Boeing.

"This idea may come to you as quite a shock but it has precedent, merit, and justice. Our accident was due plain and simple to a structural defect in the airplane. None of the hazards the flyer understands and is faced with by virtue of his chosen life – weather, mechanical malfunctions, and human errors, among others, plus, of course, acts of God – pertained in this case. So several of us thought that we could and should try to do something for the seven families. We have done this openly. Ed Nichols (author's note-Col. Edward Nichols was the Commander of the 99th Bombardment Wing, Heavy (SAC)) knew of these plans and understood our reasons therefor. And the questions now answered, it is definitely feasible.

"It goes without saying that no amount of money can ever replace a husband, father, or son. But it also follows that money, legally and rightfully acquired, can go a long way toward providing for the security of their families and education of their children. A reluctance to participate because this was Herb's life and he was proud of the part he was playing in keeping the peace has no relevance. There is absolutely no action contemplated, desired, or eve possible against the gov't, the Air Force, or any agent thereof. This is merely an action by private citizens against a private company for their product's defect.

"Wanda, no promises can be made as to the size of settlement, length of litigation, or even success. But the case is so good that the top firm in the country in this type case (Kreindler and Kreindler, 99 Park Ave, N.Y.C.-card enclosed of their representative– a former SAC pilot) has taken it on a strict contingency basis. That is, <u>all</u> the expenses and risks are theirs. If there is no favorable settlement only <u>they</u> lose. So they feel it is a darn good case. If we win they get their expenses and the usual 1/3 fee. You note I say "we". <u>I will become</u> a party in order primarily to provide necessary information and in order to establish a N.Y. jurisdiction in case Mrs. O'Keefe does not join in. (I was a New Yorker when I entered service.)

"All that is required on your part is to tell me yes or communicate directly with them. Then all that will be involved will be a signature and some information – no testimony. Then to sit back and let them handle it. Incidentally on the retained form will be name of another firm also, the referring firm. They would have a small share of the 1/3 above.

"Wanda, for your sake and for your children's as well as for Herb's, please say yes. I think Herb would have done the same for me. You can write me at the USAF Hospital, Lackland AFB, Texas.

My very best wishes to you,

(signed)Jerry Adler"

Thus, the case was built, the plaintiffs signed on, and a long wait began.

9

Questions and Answers

As soon as the crash of 0406 was confirmed, the Air Force and Boeing immediately assembled and dispatched a specialized Air Force-Industry Aircraft Accident Investigation Board to Maine. The investigators arrived at Dow during the evening hours of January 25, having been instructed to "assemble the facts surrounding the accident, analyze and evaluated the findings, and determine causes(s)." Following completion of the board's work, the Air Force Directorate of Aerospace Safety would "compile the findings of the board into one report and initiate recommendations for corrective action to preclude similar accidents."

The following morning, after being issued cold weather gear and snowshoes, the contingent of investigators travelled by bus, arriving close to the Elephant Mountain crash site, and snowshoeing the final one hundred yards. It soon became apparent that the vertical stabilizer was missing from the wreckage in the debris field. A group of three men trudged through the area together, searching for the aft section of the fuselage containing the bulkhead, designated by the number 1655, to which the vertical stabilizer had been attached. When they came upon the piece of wreckage containing that bulkhead, the vertical stabilizer's right-sided attachment lug was observed to be intact and remained bolted to the bulkhead via its attachment pin. However, the left-sided attachment lug was missing and the bulkhead was fractured at the pin's attachment site. The investigators called for a welding torch and had a twelve-inch square section of bulkhead encompassing the involved components removed for further examination.

A series of disk-like metal structures called bulkheads form the skeleton and shape of the B-52 fuselage, just as wooden framing forms the inner structure of a house. On the B-52, the sides of the disks, or bulkheads, are straight while the tops and bottoms are curved. When the plane's outer skin is attached, the fuselage assumes its characteristic shape, just as a house visually assumes its external shape after the sheathing is added. Each bulkhead is designated by a unique number that corresponds to its distance from the nose of the plane, expressed in inches. Other components of the plane may be attached to a bulkhead, just as an outdoor deck may be anchored to a house's frame. The B-52's vertical stabilizer was attached by three main fittings to the fuselage at bulkheads 1655 and 1719, 1655 inches and 1719 inches, or approximately 138 and 143 feet aft of the nose, respectively. There are two attachment fittings, or lugs, on 1655, one right-sided and one left-sided, while there is a single attachment fitting on1719.

These structures, like all others, were designed and constructed to withstand the forces that the plane was anticipated to encounter during its intended use. The B-52 was intended, and therefore designed, as a high altitude strategic bomber. The Air Force specified that the exposed area of the vertical stabilizer assembly for the B-52C should be designed to withstand side gusts generating up to 50,500 pounds of force over its 460 square feet of exposed surface. The ultimate load, or the force at which structural damage could occur, was specified as 75,700 pounds of force.

In order to meet these requirements, Boeing originally designed the upper portion of bulkhead 1655 where the vertical stabilizer attached to be constructed as a truss of heat-treated welded steel. However, it soon became apparent that the tools and methods for providing the necessary heat treatment and welding would not be in place for the first production aircraft. Therefore, the 1655 bulkheads on all three B-52A and the first six B-52B planes were fitted with a stronger and more costly crown, machined from a single forged billet, or a solid block, of aluminum alloy. The switch to a forged bulkhead was only temporary, as there was insufficient forging capacity to keep pace with aircraft production. Once adequate tooling, heat treatment, and welding became available, the originally planned steel crown was introduced. Subsequently, as forging capacity increased, aluminum forgings were reintroduced and replaced welded steel construction in several B-52 components, such as the landing gear bulkheads. Bulkhead 1655 construction, however, continued to employ welded steel. While Boeing had designed the bulkhead, it was produced by Rohr Aircraft Corporation using steel alloy from the A.O. Smith Company.

The B-52's changing mission and operating environment, along with greater than anticipated flight hours led Boeing and the Air Force to increase the frequency and breadth of inspections of structural components potentially susceptible to fatigue. One of these structures was bulkhead 1655. The inspections found small cracks developing in the steel assembly's welds. In response, Boeing issued an engineered change proposal, or ECP, designated ECP 951-0 which recommended "reinforcement of the bar connector on the upper chord of bulkhead station 1655, to prevent fatigue failure." The proposal was accepted by the Air Force on January 13, 1961, at which time it then became an Air Force Technical Order, or TO, designated TO 1B-52-1287, allowing the proposed work to progress.

A second related ECP, 951-12, was issued shortly thereafter and accepted on February 3, 1961 as TO 1B-52-1350 "to strengthen the station 1655 bulkhead to carry the fin load if cracks occur in the weld relief at waterline 240 in the bulkhead." This TO employed grinding and stop drilling to repair and prevent crack progression. The premise behind stop drilling, although at first counterintuitive, is as follows. Holes are drilled in the metal at or close to one end of a crack, without weakening the involved structure. If the crack propagates, it will reach the edge of the drilled hole and stop there. Since there is no metal in the hole, there is no material through which the crack can progress, thereby preventing crack extension.

The short interval between these technical orders was tragically interrupted on January 19, 1961 when B-52B serial number 53-0390 on a high altitude training mission over Monticello, Utah crashed with the loss of five of seven crew after severe turbulence tore off the vertical stabilizer. This incident represented the first turbulence-associated avulsion of a vertical stabilizer involving the B-52 and bulkhead 1655. It would not be the last.

The welded crown assembly of the plane's bulkhead 1655 was recovered from the wreckage and examined independently by teams from Boeing and the Air Force. Both groups determined that "the vertical fin failed first. It failed sharply to the right and contacted the horizontal stabilizer resulting in vertical fin leading edge being smashed to the left. Fin failed in a steel bulkhead adjacent to the fin terminals." Both examinations further found that "the fin failed catastrophically and there was no evidence of fatigue. Rudder and tabs still attached to fin and showed no evidence of impending failure."

The bulkhead section was then forwarded to the metallurgical laboratory of the National Bureau of Standards (NBS) in Washington, D.C. Examination and testing of the crown section was performed under the auspices of the Chief of the Mechanical Metallurgical Section, John A. Bennett. The NBS report dated April 6, 1961 concluded

"1. The primary fracture in the parts submitted had originated at a
   small fatigue crack in a weld bead.

2. The design of the part resulted in significant stress concentration,
   and this was an important factor in the initiation of the fatigue cracks.

3. A large section of the fractured member had been fabricated by
   building up the weld.

4. The relatively small growth of the fatigue crack prior to the initiation of
   fast fracture is attributed to the presence of the stress concentration

and to the very low fracture toughness of the weld metal at the operating temperature.

5. It is believed that the presence of the fatigue crack caused a significant decrease in the static strength of the part.

6. The results of the examination provide no basis for believing that this failure is unique."

The discordance between the conclusions of the NBS' report and those of Boeing and the Air Force precipitated yet a second examination of the bulkhead by both Boeing and the Air Force. Their conclusions remained unchanged, as each again determined that catastrophic failure, not fatigue cracking, had caused the welded crown truss to fracture at the vertical stabilizer's attachments. However, they did offer, "It's recognized that the sequence of failure suggested by the National Bureau of Standards is certainly possible." Even more notably, Sidney Berman, the Technical Director of the Directorate of Flight Safety Research at Norton Air Force Base in San Bernardino, California took the position of the NBS.

While the NBS' final conclusion proved prescient, the justification for its conclusion would, at best, remain arguable. Important questions remained open and unsettled. Were the observed weld cracks simply manufacturing artifacts, the normal result of the welding process that did not weaken the bulkhead at the attachment lug, enough to cause failure and detachment of the vertical stabilizer? If the cracks were "innocent bystanders" and catastrophic failure was the proximate cause of the vertical stabilizer's detachment, did the plane's original design specifications underestimate the actual wind loads to which the fin would be subjected during its planned use as a high altitude strategic bomber? Or, were the weld cracks truly manufacturing defects that did not provide sufficient strength to meet the original design specifications, rendering the bulkhead attachment susceptible to fracture under the conditions in which it was intended to be flown? Did the relatively new technique of contour flying with increased turbulence exposure have a role in exposing the bulkhead to unanticipated stresses, particularly stresses that exceeded design specifications?

Notably, neither the location of the cracks cited in the January 13, 1961 nor February 3, 1961 technical orders, nor the undertaken modifications actually involved the portion of the bulkhead that was later determined to have failed in both the Monticello accident and the loss of 0406 two years later. In fact, the two ordered modifications were performed on 0406 during March and November of 1961, respectively.

Later that year, Boeing followed up with the Air Force on the matter of bulkhead 1655, specifically the area that fractured in the Monticello crash. In a letter dated July 28, 1961 the manufacturer cited the difficulties in accessing and inspecting the portion of 1655 that was experiencing weld cracks, an issue of increasing importance given the more severe use conditions to which the B-52 was being subjected. Boeing recommended redesigning the bulkhead to be constructed from an aluminum alloy forging. Anticipated benefits over the welded steel construction included lower manufacturing costs, improved manufacturing quality control, ease of inspection in the field after installation and use, and the ability to be repaired by bolting or riveting of either metal straps or angles. The new forged units would be incorporated into all new B-52s coming off the assembly line and could be retrofitted to replace the welded steel assembly on planes already in the fleet, if required.

An Air Force representative appended the letter before it reached the designated authority for a response:

"To the best of our knowledge, the only signs of fatigue damage to the 1655 bulkhead are the area already covered by the 951 and the 951-12 fixes. We believe the cyclic testing done on the fin revealed satisfactory proof of the 951 change up to the limit of the testing done (10,000 cycle hrs.) We have never been completely convinced that 951-12 was even required, as these cracks on the cyclic test were stop drilled about midway through the test and showed no progression from the stop drilling at the end of the test. We further believe that the contractor is optomistic (sic) in saying that the cost for the new forging would compare favorable (sic) with existing part because of the limited number of parts over which the die casts would have to be amortized. Therefore, we cannot recommend the expenditure of effort on the proposed ECP."

The cyclic tests discussed in the addendum referred to ongoing static tests performed by the Air Force, in which aircraft were secured in jigs and subjected to various artificial stresses and forces over time to examine the effects on specific parts of the airframe. The Air Force replied to Boeing's request on August 30, 1961 as follows: "The referenced message requested permission to submit an ECP to accomplish the subject revision. Since this ECP could not possibly have a production effectivity (sic), the request is denied. In the event a follow on contract is authorized, this request will be reconsidered".

Boeing had also developed an ongoing flight-testing program employing several heavily instrumented B-52s that recorded over two hundred data parameters throughout the plane, including wind gust measurements. Data obtained from these flights showed that during low-level contour flying, gusts exceeding those for which the plane was designed during high altitude flight were not as rare as originally thought. Considering the B-52's growing mission as a low level penetrator, these observations raised concerns for structural damage from both overload as well as fatigue. A letter from the manufacturer to the Air Force, dated May 18, 1961 recommended several low-level training flight restrictions to mitigate these risks. The guidance included recommendations for normal and maximum airspeed, minimum and maximum gross weights, limiting low level flight to conditions of low to moderate turbulence, and exiting low level flight when severe turbulence was encountered. Two of Boeing's test plane's experienced vertical stabilizer damage during low level test flights after exceeding load limits, leading to a second, similar letter to the Air Force that was sent on June 6, 1962.

The three investigators surrounding the aft section of 0406 were Sidney Berman, the advisor to the Inspector General of the Directorate of Aerospace Safety who had been appointed as Technical Assistant to the Board President, Archie Chappel, a technical representative from the Boeing Aircraft Corporation, and Kenneth Denny, a B-52 structural engineer at the Oklahoma Air Materiel Area of Tinker Air Force Base. On Tuesday January

29, Denney, Chappel, and Berman drove to the University of Maine in Orono with the excised bulkhead segment. Seeking an expert opinion regarding the appearance of the fracture site, they located Charles Dudley Nash, Associate Professor of Mechanical Engineering. All four men took turns examining the piece with a twenty-power magnifying glass and a microscope, finding two small areas of discoloration in the fractured weld metal, which they interpreted as flaws in the weld.

While the investigators were in Orono, a six-man search team of Maine Air National Guardsmen discovered the vertical stabilizer back along the flight path near Horseshoe Pond, approximately one and one-half miles southeast of the main wreckage site. Upon returning to Greenville with their excised bulkhead section, the investigators were informed of the find and immediately headed out to inspect the fin. They found the left-sided attachment lug completely intact, with the pin that had bolted it to bulkhead 1655 still affixed.

Their observations bore an eerie resemblance to those noted in the 1961 crash of 0390. The very next day, Wednesday January 30, several members of the investigating team were urgently called away and instructed to travel immediately to the northern New Mexico town of Mora. A 52E, serial number 57-0018, had crashed after losing its vertical stabilizer in turbulence over the Sangre de Cristo Mountain range while cruising at thirty thousand feet. Two of the six crew on board perished.

The National Bureau of Standards subsequently received and examined the excised section of bulkhead 1655 from 0406. A report dated February 27, 1963, noted

"It is unusual, in a structure as complex as an airframe, to experience two failures in service that are essentially identical. The fact that this is the case in the 1655 bulkhead is noteworthy and suggests that the fracture site is markedly weaker than the associated structure. As the defects at the origin were not the same in the two cases, it does not appear that they were the only critical factors, but rather that the material is unable to tolerate even a small defect under the loading conditions imposed. Consequently there is every reason to believe that other aircraft will suffer similar failures unless corrective action is taken.

"Summary

The fracture was nearly identical to that which caused the crash at Monticello, Utah, (rest blacked out)

The fracture initiated at a defect believed to be a crack, which was present at the time of final heat treatment.

The initial part of the fracture was entirely in the weld metal.

The fracture toughness of the weld metal was much lower than that of the base steel.

The presence of the defect in the brittle weld metal caused a marked decrease in the strength of the part. It is possible that there was a cyclic crack growth beyond the bottom of the defect: this would have further reduced the load necessary to cause complete fracture of the part.

The similarity between that fracture and that from the Monticello accident indicates strongly that corrective action is essential to prevent further failures".

The NBS report, however, did not either note or comment on the specific loads or forces applied to the bulkhead during flight. Importantly, subsequent laboratory testing was conducted on the excised portion of bulkhead 1655 from 0406, specifically the intact right attachment lug. After cooling the part to -65 degrees Fahrenheit, successively loads were applied to determine the forces required to cause failure. The remaining bulkhead attachment failed only after exposure to 105% of the ultimate load, or the load at which structural failure was expected. Moreover, "failure did not occur at any existing crack." Collectively, the results of the two evaluations suggested that while the strength of bulkhead 1655 not only met, but surpassed its design specifications, the aircraft's originally anticipated operational environment, including load exposure, had been underestimated. This recognition triggered an ongoing study of atmospheric conditions, turbulence in particular, and the resultant forces to which the plane was exposed, using several B-52s loaded with instruments to collect and record the relevant information.

Together with representatives from Boeing, the Air Force urgently examined the available data regarding bulkhead 1655, and in February 1963 directed Being to immediately proceed with designing, building, and retrofitting all B-52s with a new forged aluminum bulkhead. The modification, designated ECP 1124, was deemed so critical that Boeing was requested to proceed without formal Air Force approval, which followed in April. The program cost was $41.3 million. New bulkhead installations proceeded quickly, beginning late in 1963.

While the bulkhead replacement program moved forward, an analysis of data from the atmospheric studies revealed additional critical areas of stress to the vertical stabilizer and upper fuselage. Boeing proposed strengthening these regions and presented ECP 1128 to the Air Force in September and October 1963. As with ECP 1124, the $47.1 million program was of such importance that work began before a formal contract was inked. Even more extensive than the bulkhead retrofitting, this work would prove to require several years to complete.

Despite the work pace of both ECPs, it was not fast enough to avert another bulkhead 1655 failure and vertical stabilizer detachment resulting in the loss of yet another B-52. On January 13, 1964, a B-52D, serial number 55-0060, was returning to Turner Air Force Base in Georgia after a layover at Westover following a 24-hour mission. While cruising at 30,000 feet over Pennsylvania, the plane encountered a raging blizzard. Severe turbulence avulsed the vertical stabilizer, causing the resulting crash in which three of the five crew lost their lives.

Since the fleet modifications strengthening bulkhead 1655 and the vertical stabilizer were completed, not a single life or B-52 aircraft has been lost to failure of either structure. Sadly, a total of 17 men died in peacetime service before the problem was recognized and successfully addressed. The loss of 0406 forever altered the lives of nine families, including six women who were left without their husbands, and nine children left without their fathers.

10

The Tort

Ultimately, after considering Jerry Adler's pleas, Anna O'Keefe and all surviving spouses agreed to participate in the proposed legal action against the Boeing Company. All, that is, except for Mildred Hill. Despite assurances to the contrary, she maintained that participating in the proceedings would have reflected poorly on Bob Hill's beloved Air Force.

The wheels of the justice system often grind slowly, and the case of "O'Keefe, et. al. v. The Boeing Company" was no exception. The lawsuit was filed in Federal District Court, Southern District of New York on January 23, 1964, one day shy of the first anniversary of the crash. The plaintiffs' complaint listed 18 specific allegations, collectively claiming that the crash of 0406 resulted from negligence in the design and manufacture of bulkhead 1655. Compensation was requested in the following dollar amounts:

	Wrongful death	Conscious pain and suffering
Anna M. O'Keefe	100,000	25,000
Wanda Hanson	300,000	25,000
Opel I. Morrison	300,000	25,000
Georgia J. Leuchter	300,000	25,000
Doris A. Simpson	250,000	25,000
Doris V. Gabriel	200,000	25,000
and Gerald J. Adler	400,000 for injuries based on negligence.	

The trial, however, would not begin until more than six years later, with Lee Kreindler of Kreindler and Kreindler representing the plaintiffs and James Fitz Simons of Mendes and Mount, a New York law firm specializing in aviation defense, representing The Boeing Company. The two parties agreed to plead their respective cases in a bench trial, with the trial judge serving as both judge and jury. The trial would take place in the courtroom of Judge John Matthew Cannella, who was nominated to a lifetime federal judgeship by President Kennedy on April 4, 1963, and confirmed by the Senate on June 28, 1963. Cannella had worked his way through Fordham University Law School while playing professional football for the New York Giants of the National Football League. After five years in private practice, he served as an Assistant U.S. Attorney for the Southern District of New York, and served in Coast Guard intelligence during World War II. Following the war and several appointments to various state commissions, Cannella was an Associate Justice of the New York State Court of Special Sessions up until assuming his seat on the federal bench.

The trial proceedings began in Federal District Court in Manhattan on the morning of June 1, 1970. Opening statements were given, first by Lee Kreindler, followed by James Fitz Simons. Over the ensuing days and weeks, a parade of expert witnesses appeared before Judge Cannella and was questioned by the two opposing attorneys. Structural engineers and aerospace engineers, mechanical engineers and materials engineers, metallurgists and meteorologists were presented to the court, some by the plaintiffs and others by the defense. University professors and scientists, Boeing employees and Air Force personnel all found their way to the witness stand. Jerry Adler, by now an attorney and plaintiff himself, testified and Dante Bulli's deposition was read into the record, for he was serving in Viet Nam. After a month of testimony, which generated 3452 pages of court transcripts, the trial concluded on July 2, 1970.

Judge Cannella filed his opinion on December 7, 1971, the 30th anniversary of Pearl Harbor and the 40th birthday of Jerry Adler. Following a lengthy review of the evidence and testimony presented at trial, accompanied by an explanation of his legal reasoning, Cannella opined,

"In view of the foregoing, the court is constrained to conclude that the plaintiffs have not met their burden of proof by a fair preponderance of the credible evidence that the crash of B-406 was proximately caused by the flaw at the weld relief hole. To be sure, "fact finding does not require mathematical certainty," and this rule implies that a party plaintiff's burden of proof does not involve any such requirement. However, the court finds that whatever mathematical credibility exists in this case overwhelmingly supports the defendant's theory that overload proximately caused the crash of B-406.

On the other hand, however distinguished the careers of the plaintiff's "experts" may have been and whatever their general reputations might be, the court finds the way in which they reached their conclusions in this case to have been incredibly unscientific, for the most part not because they were generally unfamiliar with the B-52, which is understandable, but because they made little, if any, effort to find out before stating their opinions at trial.

"In summarizing this opinion, which represents the court's findings of fact and conclusions of law pursuant to Rule 52 of the Federal Rules of Civil Procedure, with regard to the specific issues in the Pre-Trial Order which were tried, the court concludes that the law of Washington applies to all questions of liability, that the plaintiffs stated certain claims upon which relief could have been granted, but the claims for personal injury on the part of the decedents are barred by Washington law and the claims based upon strict liability in tort (and breach of warranty) are barred by the applicable statute of limitations. Furthermore, the court concludes that neither plaintiff Adler nor the other plaintiffs' decedents either assumed the risk of the accident or were contributorily negligent, but also that the defendant was not negligent in any respect.

"The court therefore concludes that the defendant is entitled to judgment dismissing the plaintiffs' complaint, and the parties are hereby directed to settle an order to this effect within ten days in conformity with this opinion.

"So ordered."

So ended an eight-year wait by six families and Jerry Adler to be compensated for their heart wrenching, irreplaceable losses and injuries. While appealing the court's decision was possible, after considering Judge

Cannella's opinion and the possibility that losing the appeal might incur significant financial expense to the plaintiffs, the crew's families and Jerry Adler resigned themselves to accepting the decision.

11

Memorials and Remembrances

Devastated by the crash of 0406, the Westover community rallied to provide a fitting memorial to the lost crewmen of the 99th Bombardment Wing, Heavy (SAC). Led by base commander Col. John W. Carroll, funds were raised and a stained glass memorial window was commissioned for Chapel 3, located on the air base. Designed, constructed, and installed by Whittemore and Associates of Boston, a prominent stained glass studio, the window, as described in its dedication program, "is designed around a center panel which depicts two Airmen, helmets in hand, looking off into the 'wild blue yonder' where a flight of B-52s wing their way across a cloud studded sky; the flight is missing one aircraft in honor of those memorialized. Underneath is a church on a green-wooded hillside to represent the faith of those who fly the trackless paths of the sky in the cause of freedom for all people. The shield at the top center is the insignia of the 99th Bomb Wing with its Latin motto "Caveant Aggressores" – "Aggressors Beware". The insignias, two each on the right and left sides, and three in the lower center, stand for the seven units comprising the wing. They and their mottos are:

99th Armament & Electronics Squadron

"Victory through Knowledge for Peace Tomorrow"

99th Field Maintenance Squadron

"Ready and Faithful"

99th Organizational Maintenance Squadron

"Ready and Willing"

346th Bombardment Squadron

"Never Unprepared"

347th Bombardment Squadron

McCoy AFB, Florida

348th Bombardment Squadron

"Chargers All"

24th Munitions Maintenance Squadron

"Equal to the Burden"

Maj. Al Nutter and Capt. Ken Snyder received the honor of serving as the models for the two airmen depicted in the windows, which were dedicated in front of a full chapel on the afternoon of July 17, 1964. Affixed to the bronze plaque beneath the window were the names of 0406 crew Maj. Robert J. Morrison, Maj. Robert J. Hill, Capt. Herbert L. Hanson, Capt. Charles G. Leuchter, and TSgt. Michael F. O'Keefe and two additional Westover flyers lost in separate accidents, Maj. Earl R. Cairl and SSgt. Pierre J. Maheux.

Maj. Al Nutter (lt.) and Capt. Ken Snyder (rt.) were the models for the airmen depicted in the stained glass memorial windows. (Photo courtesy of Lt. Col. Ken Snyder, USAF (ret.))

Program cover from the stained glass window dedication (Photo courtesy of Karen Adler)

The 8th Air Force relocated to Barksdale Air Force Base in Louisiana in 1970, and four years later Westover was designated as an Air Reserve Base (ARB). The status change was accompanied by a concomitant downsizing in both personnel and territory. Many of the buildings previously within the base confines were now "outside the fence", or beyond the new base perimeter, and were repurposed to house various industrial and commercial enterprises. Among these structures was the former chapel housing the windows, which was converted to the nonprofit Chicopee Child Development Center in 1979. Before relinquishing the property, the Air Force had removed the interior furnishings. During this process, plywood boards were installed, covering the exterior doors and windows, as well as the stained glass panels, which were left behind along with other memorial windows dedicated by Westover families and personnel.

Over the ensuing years, several false starts were unable to raise sufficient funds to move the collection of windows to a suitable site. Meanwhile, the stained glass' poor insulating qualities were contributing to unaffordable heating costs at the nonprofit Center. Finally, in 1988, the Armed Forces Retirement Home (AFRH) in Washington, D.C. and the Center came to an agreement that resolved both issues. The AFRH contracted with the Lizotte Glass Company of Holyoke, MA to remove, ship, restore, and reset six of the windows in the Washington, D.C facility, while installing thermal replacement windows in the Chicopee building. Additional funding provided new draperies and blinds for the Center. The entire $61,000 project concluded with a rededication of the transferred windows at the AFRH in July 1990. Although the set of windows dedicated to 0406's crew was not among those sent to Washington, D.C., as part of the overall project, it was taken down and stored at Westover. The accompanying bronze memorial plaque, however, was left behind, remaining attached to a now blank wall, devoid of any reference to its place in Westover history.

A 1990 visit to Westover by the family of Maj. Bob Morrison included a trip to the former chapel, which was sadly marked by disappointment upon finding the memorial windows absent. Max Morrison, however, observed that the bronze plaque still remained in place. Following a brief conversation, Joan Beaudry, the center's business manager, offered him to remove and take possession of the plaque, with Max fully intending to reunite it with the windows upon their reinstallation. Later receiving word that this action had caused some discontent among unknown individuals, the plaque was donated to the Moosehead Riders Snowmobile Club in Greenville, Maine in January 2003 while commemorating the fortieth anniversary of the loss of 0406. Thereafter, the whereabouts of both the windows and the plaque remained unknown to the families and friends of the men who perished on 0406. Their only tangible connections to an indelible time and place had effectively vanished.

How did a local snowmobile club become involved with preserving the memory of the crew of 0406? Late in 1992, local resident and club president, Fred Worster, determined that the group could benefit from an outside activity that would also benefit the community. A private pilot as well as an avid snowmobiler, Worster found that the upcoming thirtieth anniversary of the accident provided just such an opportunity. Over the years, some visitors had removed portions of the plane from the site as souvenirs. Yet others desecrated the sections left behind by carving them with their names or initials.

Sections of the main landing gear. After almost six decades of harsh Maine weather, the steel retains its original highly polished finish, remarkably free of rust or corrosion. (Photo by the author)

The motivating event occurred earlier in 1992. The Air Force had sold off the salvage rights to 0406, pieces of which, for the most part, remained where they had fallen. An unemployed resident of Oakland, Maine who had been performing salvage work as an income source, submitted the winning bid, and purchased the rights for the sum of $50. Unaware of the historical value and significance placed on the wreckage by area residents, he had already removed the plane's engines when he received word of the importance attached to the hallowed site. Taken aback by the outcry, he told a reporter from a local newspaper, "It turned my stomach when I found out...I didn't think anybody cared." He subsequently ceased salvage operations and turned over one of the engines retrieved from 0406's wreckage to the Moosehead Riders Snowmobile Club, where it remains on display in front of the clubhouse.

The remnants of one of 0406's eight engines salvaged from the crash site and presented to the Moosehead Riders Snowmobile Club in 1992. (Photo by the author)

The club members, working with the local American Legion, high school, and Dow Air Force Base orchestrated a two day long commemoration of the men and final flight of 0406 on January 23 and 24, 1993. The occasion culminated with a snowmobile procession to the crash site, followed by a solemn memorial service at 1452, the exact time of the accident. This event has occurred annually ever since. A five-foot tall slab of dark gray-black slate was erected and placed alongside the tail gunner's compartment in 1998, commemorating each flyer on the mission.

The tail gunner's compartment where TSgt. Mike O'Keefe served and died is the largest intact part of 0406 at the main crash site. Note the American flags surrounding a cairn of coins and pebbles left as respectful remembrances by visitors. The black slate slab memorializes each lost crewmember and honors both of the survivors. (Photo by the author)

The land on which the crash occurred represented a working forest managed and harvested by the Scott Paper Company. Through the club's efforts, Scott Paper and the land's subsequent owners, first Plum Creek Timber and later Weyerhauser, each agreed to preserve the site by excluding the area from salvage or commercial operations. Sadly, Fred Worster passed away in 1999, but his legacy continued.

Pete Pratt and his wife, Cally, both close friends of Worster and active club members, stepped up and carried on the tradition along with Fred's wife, Priscilla. Pete is particularly pleased that they were able to bring a regular military presence to the memorial ceremonies by enlisting the ongoing participation of the Maine Air National Guard. A special 50th Anniversary Commemoration was held over Memorial Day Weekend on Saturday, May 25, 2013, with services held first at the clubhouse, then at the crash site. In addition to the Moosehead Riders, participants included representatives from the Maine Warden Service, Maine Air National Guard, Greenville Police Department, American Legion, and the Boy Scouts of America. Most touchingly, invitations were extended to the surviving crew and families of those who perished. In an emotional reunion, Jerry Adler and his rescuer, Gene Slabinski, saw each other for the first time in fifty years. Due to poor health, Dan Bulli had to decline the invitation. Members of the Hanson, Hill, and O'Keefe families braved the cold downpours and accepted folded American flags from the Honor Guard. Soon after, Pete and Cally moved to Georgia and passed the torch of tending the site and arranging the annual memorial ride and service to the next generation of club members.

On January 17, 2015 the club held its annual memorial service honoring the airmen of 0406. For the first time since the tradition began, servicemen from Westover participated in the official ceremonies. Among the participants was TSgt. William Passmore, assigned to the 439th Aircraft Maintenance Squadron, who had organized the Westover presence. Having learned of the crash from other Westover personnel, he first visited the

Elephant Mountain site in 2012, a trip that would be just the first of many as Passmore dug further into the flight's history.

Gene Slabinski (lt.) and Jerry Adler (rt.) were reunited for the first time since January 25, 1963 at the Moosehead Rider's Snowmobile Club's 50th Anniversary Memorial and celebration, Memorial Day Weekend, 2013. (Photo courtesy of Theresa Bailey)

During his 2015 visit, he was made aware of a local individual who wished to relinquish possession of a unique artifact from 0406. Decades earlier, this person had been walking with a group of friends in the woods near Elephant Mountain, when he observed what appeared to be a pipe protruding from the ground. Curiosity piqued by finding such an object in the wilderness, he pulled on the metal tube and out of the ground came what appeared to be a gun barrel. This proved to be more than just a gun barrel. It was an entire Browning M2 .50 caliber machine gun, one of the four tail guns from 0406, manned by Mike O'Keefe so long ago. Severely rusted and corroded from years of exposure, the Browning was kept out of sight in its finder's garage for over twenty years. Now wishing to dispose of the gun, the individual was prepared to turn it over to Passmore, who envisioned incorporating the Browning into a monument at Westover, dedicated to 0406's crew.

Before the transfer could occur, Passmore would have to successfully navigate his way through the appropriate Air Force channels, receiving support from the base commander, legal department, and base historian to bring the tail gun back to Westover. Permissions finally in hand, the project moved forward. Dan Howard, a first sergeant at Westover who also had attended the 2015 Maine memorial service, transported the tail gun to Westover, where it was secured in the base armory. Steve Troy, an Air Force veteran and owner of Troy Industries of West Springfield, Massachusetts, volunteered to restore the Browning as a tribute to the flyers' memories. When the restoration was complete, the gun housing's top plate was engraved as the finishing touch, portraying the image of a B-52 above the crew's names.

2nd Lt. William Passmore and the salvaged .50 caliber tail gun from 0406 before its restoration and incorporation into the Westover monument. (Photo courtesy of Capt. William Passmore)

An elaborate wooden pedestal constructed for the monument's base was topped with a donated marble slab. The restored Browning was mounted to the pedestal via a metal post. Two large engraved wooden plaques were created as accompanying remembrances, the first listing the flight's crew, call sign, serial number, and the date and time of the crash. The SAC and 99th

Bomber Wing insignias and mottos flanked the text. The second plaque recounted 99th Bomber Wing, Heavy (SAC) Commander Col. O. F. Lassiter's foreword written for "Sky Sentry-A SAC Crewman in Service," featuring Mike O'Keefe's story, and published in 1959 by Arnold Brophy. The completed monument's dedication ceremony was held at Westover on June 4, 2016.

The completed .50 caliber tail gun monument (Photo by the author)

In April of 2019, Hector Torres Camacho, Ph.D., arrived at Westover ARB in the full-time role of base historian. Notably, he had first hand experience in the Air Force, serving as an enlisted airman prior to completing his undergraduate degree and graduate education in history. After learning the story of 0406, including the missing memorial windows and accompanying tablet, he confirmed that not only were the stained glass memorial windows still in the local area, but that in the spring of 1996 they had been removed from storage and reinstalled in Westover ARB's Chapel 1 located in Building 1100, the original airfield's headquarters building. However, the accompanying bronze plaque was nowhere to be found.

The stained glass windows memorializing the crew of 0406 and two other Westover officers who perished in separate flight accidents, currently installed in the Westover ARB Chapel 1. The airmen depicted to the left and right, respectively, represent the likenesses of Maj. Al Nutter and Capt. Ken Snyder. (Photo by the author)

A June 2019 visit to Greenville, Maine included The Center for Moosehead History's Moosehead Lake Aviation Museum. There, an exhibit dedicated to preserving the story of the crash filled a small room. Among the collection of documents and artifacts was a bronze plaque affixed to one wall. The tablet was unidentified and further obscured behind a display case containing Dan Bulli's repacked parachute. On closer inspection, the names of the seven Westover flyers originally memorialized by the stained glass windows were clearly visible. The missing memorial plaque had been located.

How did the plaque arrive at this surprising location? The Moosehead Riders Snowmobile Club, which for years served in Greenville as the local repository and caretaker of artifacts and memorabilia related to the crash of 0406, had closed its building's doors in 2017 when the adjacent access-providing snowmobile trails were closed by neighboring landowners. Although the club remained active, with no place to store or display the crash-related items, the Moosehead Riders relinquished the collection, including the memorial window dedication plaque, to the local historical society, which operated The Center for Moosehead History. After being informed of the plaque's location and significance, and asked if its return to Westover would be supported, Torres Camacho responded, "I can speak for Westover and say that we would accept the plaque to be with the windows."

The mission to reunite the plaque with the windows at Westover continued with enthusiastic assent of the families of 0406's memorialized men. Upon learning the plaque's origin and significance, Suzanne Au Clair, Executive Director of The Center for Moosehead History, graciously agreed to transfer the plaque from the aviation museum to Westover ARB. She wrote to Torres Camacho, "The Moosehead Historical Society would like to return this plaque to you to be displayed with the stained glass window in commemoration of the B-52 crew…We're very pleased to be able to return this item in honor of the men of the B-52, and to know it won't be lost and people will see it."

On September 27, 2019, Au Clair completed the paperwork officially removing the object from the society's collection in preparation for delivery to Westover. The casting's cold hardness recalled the harsh fates befalling the men whose names were affixed to its burnished surface, its ample weight a reminder of their survivors' heavy hearts. The plaque was returned to Westover on October 30, 2019, placed in the hands of Torres Camacho and TSgt. Shane Phipps of the base public affairs office, and delivered to Chapel 1, where it was mounted adjacent to the stained glass windows on November 1, 2019. The 439th Airlift Wing commemorated the event with a rededication ceremony held on November 4, 2019.

Nothing could ever extinguish the pain and loss experienced by those close to the flyers who perished on January 24, 1963. However, in the weeks and months following the tragedy of 0406, the stained glass memorial windows and accompanying memorial plaque had provided a focus for both the Westover community's collective grief and for healing. Reuniting these two pieces more than three decades after they were separated, relocated, and believed lost, restored a source of comfort as originally envisioned so many years before, closing the final chapter recounting the final mission of 0406 and her Westover crewmen.

The bronze plaque naming the Westover flyers memorialized by the accompanying stained glass windows was returned to Westover ARB on October 30, 2019. Receiving the plaque were TSgt. Shane Phipps of the Westover public affairs office (lt.), and Hector Torres Camacho, Ph. D., base historian (rt.). (Photo by the author)

12

Epilogue

Col. Dante Eugene Bulli, USAF (Ret.)

Dan Bulli transferred to Maxwell Air Force Base in Alabama shortly after being released from medical care for his injuries incurred in the crash of 0406. Accompanied by his family, he spent one year studying at the Air War College. Once fully recovered, he maintained his flight status by flying the C-47, a World War II era military version of the DC-3 twin propeller aircraft. After leaving Maxwell, Bulli was back in the cockpit of B-52s and promoted to Colonel while stationed at McCoy Air Force Base in Florida, eventually seeing combat duty in Viet Nam. He was permanently grounded after experiencing a stroke at age 45 while assigned to Loring Air Force Base in Limestone, Maine. After a lengthy recovery, Bulli was able to remain on active duty as a senior officer in Air Force SAC Intelligence until his retirement in 1974 after more than thirty years of service covering three wars.

He and Ev remained in Nebraska until her passing at age 90 on September 13, 2015 and his death on December 30, 2016 at age 94. They are buried together in their hometown of Cherry, Illinois. Dan designed their shared grave marker. Ev's memorial, topped by the engraved image of an open book, reads "Faithful wife, Loving mother, Respected educator, World traveler." Dan's epitaph, topped by the engraving of a B-52 in profile, remembers him as "Faithful husband, Caring father, Skilled aviator, Veteran of WWII, Korean & Viet Nam wars".

Dan Bulli following his 1964 promotion to Colonel and assignment as Commander, 367th Squadron, 306th Bombardment Wing at McCoy AFB, Florida. (Photo courtesy of John Bulli)

Their son, John, graduated from the University of Illinois and works as an advertising account manager for local media outlets. He and his family reside in Illinois, not far from Cherry. Marilyn graduated with a doctorate in music and teaches voice in the Boston area.

Capt. Gerald Jay Adler, USAF (Ret.)

Following his medical retirement, Jerry rejoined his family in Sonya's hometown of Houston where he attended law school, graduating from the University of Houston in 1966. He continued his studies, receiving master's degrees in international law from New York University and Columbia University. In 1968, Jerry was recruited to the founding faculty of the University of California at Davis School of Law. He remained on the faculty until 1974, when he entered the private practice of law, retiring in 2007. During those years, Jerry was elected to the Davis City Council, serving from 1980-1992 including a term as Mayor in 1990. Jerry and Sonya adopted a son, Jonathan Charles, who serves his local community assisting those afflicted by substance abuse. His middle name was given in memory of Capt. Charles Leuchter. Sonya passed away in 2007. Jerry later married author Nancy Tesler, a long-time friend and the younger sister of his college roommate. They currently live in northern California.

Adler's efforts to ensure a lifetime of guidance, support, and resources for the six widows and nine children of 0406's lost crew would simultaneously become both a lifelong touchstone and personal grail. Disappointed with the 1970 trial's outcome, he experienced nagging doubts as to whether he had lived up to his personal commitment made so many years before. Had he done enough and could he have done more for those families? Shari Morrison Hovey offered a clear and pointed response addressing his self-questioning. "He kept his word as far as I am concerned."

Jerry Adler and Nancy Tesler celebrating Jerry's birthday, December 7, 2014. (Photo courtesy of Karen Adler)

SMSgt Eugene Slabinski, USAF (Ret.)

Eugene Slabinski remained on active duty until September 1, 1976 and continued his military career in the active reserves until his retirement at the rank of Senior Master Sergeant (SMSgt.) on July 4, 1978 with over twenty-eight years of service. Slab then obtained his nursing degree from Lucerne County Community College in 1979 and enjoyed a second career in psychiatric nursing until retiring in the early 1980's. Five of his eight children have served in the United States military. He notes with a chuckle, "We had a girls basketball team with three boys for reserves." With respect to Dan Bulli's thank you gift, he offered, "I quit smoking a long time ago, but I still have that lighter." He currently volunteers at a local Veterans Administration Hospital near his home in western Pennsylvania and regularly travels throughout Canada and the United States to attend pararescuer unit reunions.

Bulli, Adler, and Slabinski would remain in contact with each other for the rest of their lives, sharing family events including weddings and funerals, exchanging holiday greetings, and talking by telephone – not surprisingly on or around January 25th of every year.

SMSgt Eugene Slabinski, USAF (Ret.) with his engraved lighter, a thank you gift from Dan Bulli, undated. (Photo courtesy of Karen Adler)

The Hansons

Wanda Hanson, Capt. Herb Hanson's widow, returned home to Rapid City, South Dakota. Assisted by her parents, Moraha and Fred Dean, she joined the family catering business, Pretty Pines Party House, supporting and raising her three daughters. Wanda, though very intelligent, did not have the opportunity to advance her education beyond high school and had not developed a set of marketable work skills. Pressed by her mother to remarry as a means of improving financial support for her family, Wanda followed suit. Sadly, the marriage did not work out and ended in divorce. Determined that her daughters would not face an uncertain future, she ensured that sufficient funds were saved for their higher educations. Wanda would not remarry again and passed away in 2004.

Wanda Hanson working at Pretty Pines Party House, undated. (Photo courtesy of Deana and Gary Packingham)

Deana, the oldest of the three Hanson daughters, and Gary Packingham tried to continue their relationship long distance. Difficult under any circumstances, the endeavor was even harder in the days before cell phones and easily accessible air travel. College and new relationships intervened and the two drifted apart. Deana graduated from the University of Wyoming with a degree in nursing, and practiced for many years. Nevertheless, the former high school steadies always remained in touch. Eventually, good fortune would intervene, bringing Deana and Gary together in marriage later in life. The couple now resides in Michigan.

Trish, the Hansons' middle daughter, attended Colorado State University, graduating with a B.S. in home economics. After working in retail and as a model, she has been employed for the past 20 years by a nonprofit community services management corporation. She shared that, "I realize now that my dad's death really did have a profound effect on my life…it took me many years to really go through the grieving period. When my mom and her second husband got divorced, it was sort of as if I felt abandoned once again." Trish lives with her husband in Maryland, close to her three children and four grandchildren.

Herb and Wanda's youngest daughter, Sam, like her oldest sister graduated college with a nursing degree. She specialized in neonatal intensive care nursing, caring for the youngest, tiniest, and most ill newborn infants. In retirement, she hones her skills as a master gardener, and lives with her family in South Dakota.

Before his death, Herb had been selected for promotion to the rank of Major. After Wanda and her parents lobbied both the Air Force and South

Dakota Senator George McGovern, Herb was posthumously promoted to Major, although Wanda and the girls would only receive the benefits due a Captain. His headstone notes his final rank.

The Hills

Mildred Hill, Maj. Robert Hill's spouse, moved back to Joplin, Missouri to be close to both sides of their family and raise their daughter. Mildred passed away in 2013. Daughter Roberta ("Bobbie") graduated Joplin High School and went on to be one of the top four graduates in her college class. Bobbie would teach high school geography and Spanish for thirty years. Now retired from teaching, she currently lives in Missouri and continues her lifelong love of animals, caring for a multitude of rescue cats and dogs.

Bobbie (lt.) and Mildred (rt.) celebrating Christmas at home in Joplin, Missouri, undated. (Photo courtesy of Roberta Hill)

The O'Keefes

Michael's younger sister Agnes, pregnant at the time of his death, gave birth to a healthy baby girl named Michele Frances Patricia in his memory. Anna O'Keefe, TSgt. Michael O'Keefe's mother, remained in New York City near her surviving children until her death in 1985 at the age of 83. Richard, who was tasked with serving as the intermediary between the Air Force, Anna, and other family members, passed away in 2019 at the age of 90. Until the end, he still could recount the tragic events of January 1963 with complete clarity and accuracy. Richard kept the two notification telegrams informing him of Michael's missing status and death inside the cover of his Bible on a shelf next to his bed.

Anticipating flying the next series B-52, in which the tail gunner position would be moved to the forward crew cabin with its own upward ejection seat, with his characteristic good humor, Mike had explained to author Arnold Brophy, "It is going to be wonderful to see other pretty faces around you in the aircraft." He never got the chance.

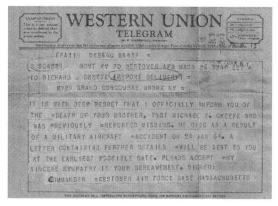

The telegram received by Richard O'Keefe on January 26, 1963 notifying him of Michael's death. (Photo courtesy of Theresa Bailey)

Richard O'Keefe visiting the shared gravesite of his father, John, and brother, Mike, at the Long Island National Cemetery in Farmingdale, New York, 2007. (Photo courtesy of Theresa Bailey)

The Morrisons

Irene Morrison, the widow of Maj. Robert Morrison, moved to the Orlando, Florida area with their two children to be close to many of her friends whose husbands had been reassigned to McCoy Air Force Base, which today is the site of Orlando International Airport. The proceeds from Bob's life insurance policy provided Irene with the means to purchase a home for her family. Ken Snyder, Morrison's co-pilot and good friend who

169

broke the news of the plane's accident to the family, visited regularly from Westover, watching over Irene and the children. They soon fell in love, married, and together had a son, Mark.

Daughter Shari noted that while Irene "was a great Air Force wife, she was very happy when Ken retired from the Air Force. She no longer had to worry when he was flying." Ken and Irene shared fifty-two years together until her passing in 2016. Shari added, "We love Ken Snyder. He is a great person and has always been there for us. He was the perfect husband for our mother. She loved him as much as he loved her. They had a wonderful marriage. I am so thankful that he has been, and still is, in our lives." She and her husband divide their time between Florida and Cape Cod.

Her brother expressed a similar sentiment, stating that Ken was always "a wonderful, wonderful guy." Max reflected on his father, "When I turned thirty six, I thought for sure I wasn't going to live out the year…it's just hard to look back at him being thirty six and dying so young." Thanks to Max, Robert James Morrison's name lives on through his grandson. Snyder retired as a Lieutenant Colonel after twenty years of service and resides in northern California where he and Mark own and operate a shop specializing in Asian art and home furnishings.

The Leuchters

Georgia Leuchter, Capt. Charles Leuchter's widow, settled in northern California. She managed to continue her nursing career while struggling to raise their two children. Sadly, Georgia never fully recovered from the loss of her husband and passed away in 2003.

13

Afterword

The telling of the story of the last flight of B-52C serial number 53-0406, or Frosh 10, her call sign on January 24, 1963, represents the culmination of a remarkable team effort that stretched from Maine to California, from Michigan to Missouri, and from Maine to Florida. I will forever be indebted to the airmen and their families who, from the start, responded positively to the concept of this work. They freely opened their homes and hearts, and willingly shared lifetimes of memories marked by joy and fulfillment and sadly, pain and loss that still ache to this very day. No words can adequately express the thanks due for their encouragement, support, and dedication to bringing this work to a successful conclusion.

Much to my disappointment, all efforts to locate and contact the families of Lt. Col. Joe Robert Simpson, Jr. and Maj. William Walter Gabriel were unsuccessful. The resulting omissions are my responsibility alone and remain a source of ongoing regret. I offer my sincere apologies to their families and hold out hope that someday relatives and former fellow flyers might come across this volume and reach out so that their stories can be told.

Additional thanks are due the many individuals who patiently and cheerfully answered my many letters, emails, and phone calls while the research behind this work was underway. Their willingness to go above and beyond cleared many potential roadblocks, which would unexpectedly pop up periodically.

The purpose of this writing was to honor the lives and memories of the January 24, 1963 flyers on 0406's final mission and to provide an appropriate remembrance for their families. It should in no way be misconstrued as "pointing fingers" or finding fault with the actions or decisions made by the United States Air Force, Boeing Aircraft Corporation, or the pilots and crew of that tragic flight. Those determinations were made long ago and are reflected in the findings of the joint military-industry accident investigation board and Judge John Matthew Cannella's 1971 decision in O'Keefe v. Boeing Company, United States District Court, Southern District of New York.

As so often happens in the cases of tragic accidents, no one factor was or can be implicated as "the" direct cause of the loss of 0406 and her crew– not the manufacture or maintenance of the aircraft, not the low level contour flight strategy, not the delayed takeoff for ACR maintenance, not the delayed departure for local ACR calibration, not the discordance between the local Westover weather reports and the actual local Westover weather, not the decision to fly the northern route (which resulted from the preceding factors), not the slight course departure to train over Elephant Mountain, and not the winds and resulting turbulence over the mountain on that January afternoon. Rather, a "perfect storm" had to befall the flight with each of these factors and events occurring in an odds-defying temporal and geographic sequence.

With the benefit of hindsight, it stands to reason that the vertical stabilizer failures and associated crashes with loss of life that included 0406 could have been avoided had bulkhead 1655 been replaced sooner as recommended in July of 1961, since no further failures occurred after the modifications covered by ECPs 1124 and 1128 were integrated into the fleet. At the time, however, that decision was not at all clear. First, manufacturing capacity for the proposed replacement was limited by both equipment and the need to fulfill the Air Force's remaining B-52 orders, which was a matter of utmost national security at the time. Second, as only one accident attributable to a bulkhead failure happened before July 1961 and that investigation's conclusions regarding the role of the bulkhead were conflicting, at that juncture the Air Force's decision appeared reasonable and appropriate. Moreover, it must be remembered that the B-52 fleet comprised the largest of three components of the United States' strategic nuclear deterrence, the other two being land-based missiles and submarine-based missiles. Taking the fleet of aircraft offline for modifications during a period of extreme tension with the Soviet Union on the heels of the Cuban Missile Crisis would have been inconceivable.

Only later, following the loss of 0406, would it become clear that while the bulkhead 1655's construction met design and manufacturing specifications set by the Air Force and Boeing, and was able to tolerate the specified loads for which it was designed, the actual forces encountered during both the originally intended and subsequent evolving mission requirements exceeded the part's ultimate construction tolerances, leading to the vertical stabilizer detachments.

The facts, as best as I can discern almost sixty years later are presented herein, and reflect a compilation of the newspaper reports of the time, court transcripts, official Air Force documents, personal correspondence and recollections of Air Force personnel, the crew of 0406 and their family members, and their personal recollections, documents, artifacts, memorabilia, and photographs.

Joseph R. Wax

October 31, 2019

Acknowledgements

With heartfelt gratitude and immeasurable thanks to

-Capt. Gerald "Jerry" Jay Adler, USAF (Ret.) and family (Karen Adler, Sheree Adler Blundell, Nancy Tesler)

-SMSgt. Eugene Slabinski, USAF (Ret.) and family (Dolores Moleski)

-Lt. Col. Kenneth Snyder, USAF (Ret.)

-Lt. Col. Florian Richard Neveu, USAF (Ret.)

-The family of Col. Dante Eugene Bulli, USAF (Ret.) (John Bulli, Marilyn Bulli)

-The family of Maj. Herbert Lawrence Hanson, USAF (Deana Lynn Hanson Packingham, Patricia Jane Hanson Shipley, Samantha Carol Hanson, Gary Packingham)

-The family of Maj. Robert James Hill, Jr., USAF (Opal Fay Hill Boyd, Roberta "Bobbie" Hill)

-The family of Maj. Robert James Morrison, USAF (Sharan "Shari" Morrison Hovey and R. Max Morrison)

-The family of TSgt. Michael Francis O'Keefe, USAF (Theresa O'Keefe Bailey, Ken Bailey, Richard O'Keefe)

-Brig. Gen. James R. "Russ" McCarthy, USAF (Ret.)

-Maj. Tommy Towery, USAF (Ret.)

-Capt. William Passmore, USAF, 439th Air Lift Wing, Westover ARB

-Hector Torres-Camacho, Ph.D., Base Historian, 439th Air Lift Wing, Westover ARB

-TSgt. Shane Phipps, USAF, Public Affairs Office, 439th Air Lift Wing, Westover ARB

-Suzanne Au Clair, Executive Director, The Moosehead Historical Society Center for Moosehead History, Greenville, Maine

-Joan Beaudry, Chicopee Child Development Center, Chicopee, Massachusetts

-Bruce Bowden

-Steve Campbell, Northern Timbers Cruisers Snowmobile Club, Millinocket, Maine

-Suzanne Cordes

-Michael Dignan, South Paris, Maine Public Library

-Kelley Mcannaney, United States National Archives, New York, New York

-Betsy Paradis, Bangor, Maine Public Library

-Pete Pratt, Moosehead Riders Snowmobile Club, Greenville, Maine

-Elizabeth Stevens, Bangor, Maine Public Library

-Brett Stolle, Curator, National Museum of the United States Air Force

-Dagney Villegas, Indianapolis, Indiana Public Library

-Rapid City, South Dakota Society for Genealogy Research

-B-52 Stratofortress Association

From The Portland (Maine) Press Herald (with permission):

"Routine Training"

"The plane was on a routine training flight."

"How many times do we read that statement? So many times it is included in an account of a tragedy, a plane that never completed its routine mission. We saw and heard those words last week here in Maine when a big jet bomber of the Strategic Air Command settled helplessly out of the sky and dipped to its destruction against the frozen side of a Northern Maine mountain.

"It carried men to a desolate death in a land as strange to then as the sands of the Sahara or a swamp in Viet Nam. For others, there was pain and shock and hours of uncertainty, but there was rescue.

"So are men sacrificed in the search for peace year after year. To do the job, which is the ultimate purpose of their service, they must be prepared as every other man is prepared to practice his craft. Essential to that preparation are experienced men, the teachers and leaders. Essential to (sic) are routine training missions.

"Often we watch in fascination as a big SAC jet finger paints on a blue sky, the setting sun sometimes turning the graceful lines into brilliant orange and gold patterns. Many of these planes, we suppose, are on routine training flights. Any of them, we know, could suffer the fate that overtook the craft from Westover last week.

"A nation usually recognizes its debt to is fighting men. It sometimes overlooks the fact that the debt exists although the men aren't fighting. It's a standing obligation because the routine training flight is a kind of combat mission. The consequences can be the same."

Wings of Freedom

Aloft a giant silverbird I see
With wings of hammered steel,
Ripping through the fleece-lined clouds;
Its graceful pace and contrails white
Make cobweb lace across the sky.
Sometimes though the clouds are gray
And chilling winds and icy snows
Like silvery fingers choke the sky
A thundering explosion sends
Men hurtling into a bed of snow.
Some will live - Some will die
And in the calm awakening of life renewed
A gentle wind on the trees doth sing-
"Peace of Earth-let freedom ring."

-Sonnie Adler

Joseph R. Wax

Final Resting Places of the Lost Crewmen of Frosh One Zero

Lt. Col. Joe R. Simpson
Barrancas National Cemetery
Pensacola, Florida

Major William W. Gabriel
Golden Gate National Cemetery
San Bruno, California

Major Robert J. Morrison
Maple Grove Cemetery
Dodge City, Kansas

Major Robert J. Hill
Osborne Memorial Cemetery
Joplin, Missouri

Major Herbert L. Hanson
Black Hills National Cemetery
Sturgis, South Dakota

Captain Charles G. Leuchter
Golden Gate National Cemetery
San Bruno, California

TSgt. Michael F. O'Keefe
Long Island National Cemetery
Farmingdale, New York

Made in the USA
Monee, IL
05 October 2020

43991005R00109